DRAMA
MADE
EASY

A Complete Step by Step Handbook for Producing Skits and Plays

Karena Krull

Published by Eternal Hearts
P.O.Box 107
Colville,WA 99114
509-732-4147

Published by: Eternal Hearts
            P O Box 107
            Colville, WA 99114

Phone: (509) 732-4147
Fax: (509) 732-4147

ISBN 0-9651342-0-2

Printed in the U.S.A.

Acknowledgements

First I want to thank Jesus, for He is the reason for my writing. The patience and compassion He has shown me while producing this book, and in my life, never cease to amaze me. Thank you, Lord, for being the author and finisher of my life.

I also want to thank the following people who supported and helped me with writing this book:

Lizabeth Brasells for editing, answering questions about the content, and more editing! Her moral support was invaluable!

Jan Bunger for being a faithful friend and by reading this book from a novice's perspective, thereby giving me reassurance that the book lived up to its title.

Marie MacDonald for being my mentor and believing in me years ago.

Ellyn Roe for taking time to check the accuracy of the book's contents after she had <u>just</u> completed a <u>huge</u> play production in my church.

Sherry Wallmark for editing this book and reading it from a novice's perspective. Her encouraging words were wonderful.

My children, Tay Adam, Rachael, and Branden, for their understanding and uncomplaining patience while I wrote.

My husband, Tay, for encouraging me to write this book. He supported me by grocery shopping and running the kids to baseball and 4-H. His cooking our many meals was invaluable. I want to thank him especially for being my best friend.

<u>Last but not least</u>, I'd like to thank my dear friend and business partner Sandra Everson. Our company was named Eternal Hearts because our hearts have made us friends for over twenty years, and we will be friends forever through our belief in Jesus Christ. Her countless hours with helping produce this book and her willingness to read my "hieroglyphics" without complaint (if handwriting were an indicator, I would have made a great doctor) were appreciated more than she will ever know. Without her support and friendship, the joy of writing this book would not exist!

Thanks again to everyone,

Karena Krull

Art Credits:
Desk Gallery Image Collection   © 1994 Zedcor Inc.
Mac Gallery Special Edition   © 1994 Dream Maker Software

Cover Designs:
Martyn Illustration & Graphics, Renton WA

Preface

I have always enjoyed drama. I still remember at age twelve, my excitement and anticipation when the curtain began to rise on a high school production of "My Fair Lady". My three older siblings all had parts in the production. In the orchestra my sister played her viola and on stage my two brothers were actors. When the curtain descended its final time, my heart could have "danced all night"!

Years later I began producing skits I had written for my church. Though I was naive, slowly but surely I learned the different aspects and problems of producing plays. My experience taught me four things I would like to pass on to you before you begin this book.

1) God does not ask for perfection, but He uses people with willing hearts as His vessels. I know because He has used me. I remember coming home from rehearsal one night, not having a clue how to **fix** a particular scene. For two days no answer came. In honest despair, I reminded God, quite pointedly, that this was His play. If He didn't give me the answer, I was no longer responsible--He was! Funny thing, once God was in control again, the answer quickly came!

2) Drama is a tremendous outreach to the audience and that is the reason we choose to produce a play. But many times a new director is unaware of the impact and growth that will occur *within* the people taking part in the production. I have had great pleasure seeing people improve their public speaking skills, gain personal confidence, and learn the co-operation and flexibility only drama can teach.

3) Don't be afraid to stretch your comfort zone. I recently volunteered to help put makeup on fifty choir members who were angels in my church's Easter event. I was inexperienced in this area but felt I could help apply any makeup except the foundation (the stuff you put on the actor's entire face and neck). You guessed it! God stretched my comfort zone and I did foundation, foundation, and more foundation!

4) My final advice is to be prepared to work hard, be flexible, and pray without ceasing for the audience who will see the performance, as well as those helping in any part of the production. If God is calling you to put on plays, remember, "I (you) can do all things through Christ who strengthens me (you)." (Phillipians 4:13).

God Bless Always,
In All Ways!

Karena Krull

Table of Contents

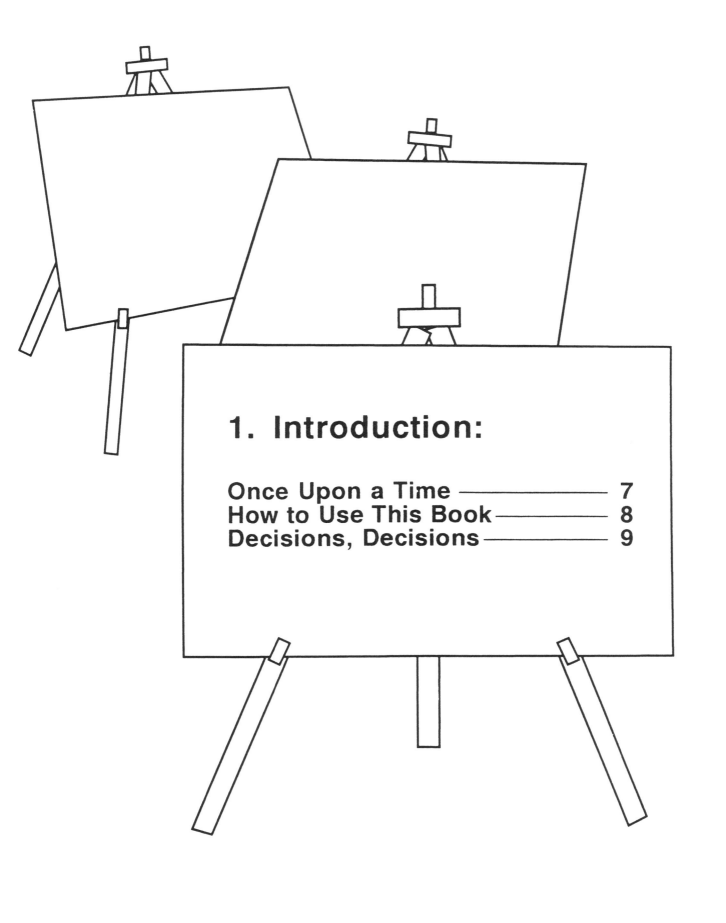

1. Introduction:

Once upon a time in the land of Drama, there lived a Prince named Director. One day, Prince Director decided to travel to the "Province of Performance". He summoned his most loyal and trusted subjects, Stage Manager and Business Manager. Together they planned and mapped out the different paths they would take to the "Province of Performance", deciding they would rendezvous in the town of "Run Through" in six weeks. With great expectations and excitement, they all set out on their journey.

Prince Director employed many Actors as he traveled through the town of "Audition". He instructed the Actors to meet in the town of "Rehearsal" in one week's time and bring their "memorized lines" with them. But, alas, a week passed by and many of the Actors were not only late to arrive, but most had not brought their "memorized lines".

Discouraged with the Actors' lack of commitment, our Prince was still determined to reach "Performance" on time. He stayed many weeks in the town of "Rehearsal", working harder than ever, until the Actors were ready to travel to the town of "Run Through".

Late, tired, and weary, Prince Director arrived in the town of "Run Through". "Surely," sighed the Prince, "the worst of my journey is now behind me. I will meet with my loyal subjects Stage Manager and Business Manager. Together, we will go on to the 'Province of Performance'."

Oh, our poor naive Prince, he had never traveled the road to "Performance" before. He had no way to know the perils that had befallen his loyal subjects on their different paths. Stage Manager had not found his provisions (props) along the way. Nor did the clothing (costumes) fit the Actors. And POOR Business Manager ...when he heard what the journey had cost, he collapsed into a dejected heap mumbling "Why me?" under his breath.

Prince Director sat down and contemplated his dilemma. What had gone wrong? What could or should he do now? Why had he desired to travel to the "Province of Performance" in the first place? It was too late to turn back and go home. Announcements of his arrival in "Performance" had already been delivered to all the people in the land. Where, oh where, was his "Happy Ending"?...

Well, my friend, don't fret for Prince Director and his loyal subjects. After working very hard and pulling together, they lived happily and more wisely ever after in the "Province of Performance".

The moral of this Fairy Tale is that each journey you make to the "Province of Performance" will have problems! My hope for you is that by reading Drama Made Easy, you will understand the journey you are about to embark on. With appropriate prayer, planning, communication, and commitment, you will avoid the "surprises" and "disappointments" Prince Director encountered.

Thus... Drama Made Easy!

How to Use This Book

Drama Made Easy was designed to be thorough, yet easy to follow and understand. We have printed on one side only, of each page, to leave you space for your own notes and ideas.

The first nine chapters of the book give you background knowledge so the skits will be easy to understand when you produce them.

These chapters include:
- how to plan
- how to organize
- steps to producing a play
- description of makeup and how to apply it
- miscellaneous ideas and advice to help you with stage fright, voice, where to locate items, etc.
- a glossary
- reproducible sheets and checklists for organization and planning (see copyright)

Chapter ten contains two skits with everything needed to produce them. Included with each skit are the Director's notes, sample schedule, and a list of costumes, props, and makeup.

The last chapter contains various resources that may be of interest to you, included are books on various drama subjects, addresses of the makeup companies, and more.

I have used the pronoun "he" instead of he/she, throughout the book for the sake of time. (My typing is slow enough as it is!)

I recommend that you tab each chapter of the book. Suggested tab titles are as follows:
- Planning
- Organization
- Production
- Technical Stuff
- Makeup
- Miscellaneous Ideas and Help
- Glossary
- Reproducible Production Sheets
- Checklists
- "Willing Obedience" Skit
- "Visitor In "Missionaryland" Skit
- Resources

Decisions, Decisions

So you want to put on a play! Great! Producing a play can be a wonderful experience, bringing people together to work toward a single purpose, and creating fantastic camaraderie. Or, plays can easily become frustrating and negative, pulling people apart. The differences that separate the outcomes are sufficient prayer, planning, commitment, good communication, and flexibility.

So before you dive in . . .

please consider
the Planning and Organization
sections carefully!

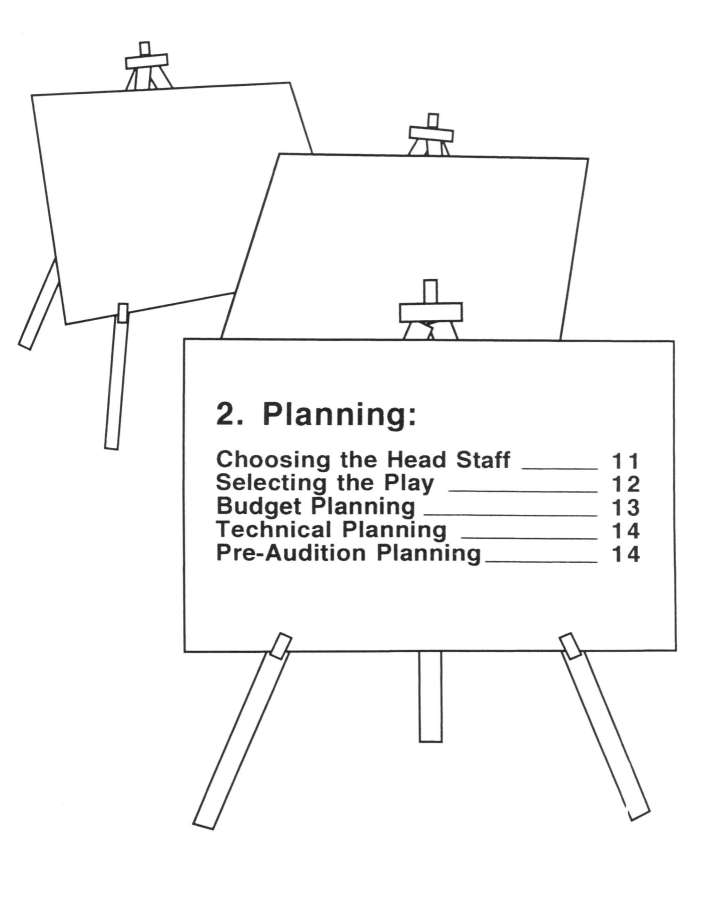

2. Planning:

CHOOSING THE HEAD STAFF:

The Head staff is in charge of the different production aspects. Below is a list of the ideal staff needed to put on a production along with a brief description of their jobs. (Chapter 2 has a complete description of all production leads and their crews.)

Producer - oversees the entire production and makes sure everything is proceeding on schedule

Director - works with the actors, develops the play, and works with the different production crews on his visions of makeup, costumes, scenes, etc.

Business Manager - is in charge of all the finances, publicity, programs, and ushers

Technical Director - oversees lighting, sound, and set design

Stage Manager - works closely with the Director. Is in charge of all stage and backstage situations, costuming, and makeup.

If you choose to perform Musical drama, a Music Director will be needed to work with the soloists, ensembles, and musicians.

If there is dancing, a choreographer will be needed.

If you do not have enough people to staff all the positions, see page 17 for alternative ideas. For the purpose of this book (and to ease your stress) we will use the ideal given above.

SELECTING THE PLAY:

– When deciding on a play to perform, you need to consider which type of play interests you:

- **Tragedies** are dramas centered on unhappy events or powerful struggles
- **Comedies** are humorous
- **Historical** plays depict different time periods and stories
- **Thrillers** have suspense or mystery plots
- **Musicals** can be any of the plays above with singing, dancing, and/or music. Not all Musicals include all three.

– Consider the purpose of the play. To:

- entertain
- teach
- make a statement
- provoke thought
- other

– Consider your audience:

- friends
- family
- church
- community

– How long will the play be? (three minutes, twenty, or more?)

– How many weeks do you have to prepare for the final performance? (two weeks, six weeks, or two months?)

– How many people do you have to put on the play? (actors, production people, etc.)

– Where will it be performed?

- home
- school
- church
- theater

BUDGET PLANNING:

The Business Manager meets with the Director and other head staff to discuss the following:

- What is the source for the money to produce and perform the play?

    - donations
    - cast
    - community
    - ticket sales
    - freewill offering
    - concessions
    - fund-raisers
    - church
    - other

- Budget costs for the play:

    - royalties to perform the play
    - rights to the play (if applicable)
    - purchased scripts or photocopies of script, if legal
    - publicity
    - costumes
    - makeup
    - props
    - sets
    - programs
    - lighting
    - sound
    - tickets
    - theater rental
    - janitor services

13

TECHNICAL PLANNING:

(Decide which if any of the following you will need for your production.)

- lighting

- sound effects

- props

- set/scenery

- video tape and/or camera shots of performance

- curtain

PRE-AUDITION PLANNING:

- Director studies the play and decides how to express the theme using the actors, costumes, sets, props, etc.

- Director decides how he desires to portray the conflicts, suspense, and climax of the plot.

- Director develops the characters and their relationships to each other.

- Director chooses props and/or furniture that create the feeling or mood of each scene.

- Director makes copies of the Audition Questionnaire before the audition (see page 70).

- Director announces the time, date, and what to bring, if necessary, to the audition. (Some Directors ask the actor to bring a prepared monologue to read, or music to sing if doing a musical. Most Directors prefer the actual script or songs.)

Still contemplating diving in?

Discover how jobs are organized in the next chapter.

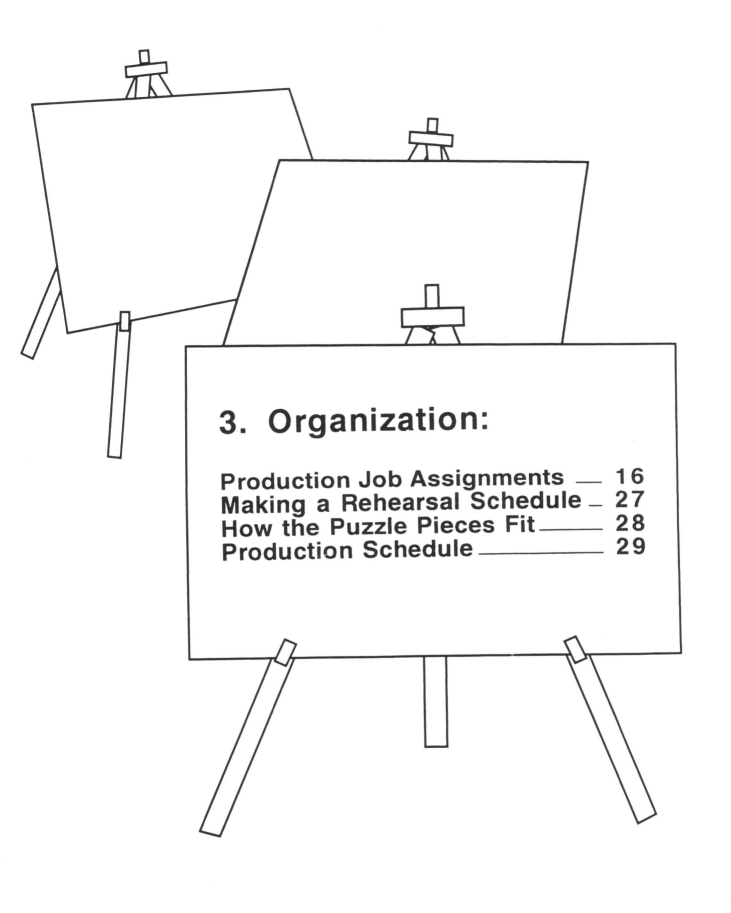

3. Organization:

PRODUCTION JOB ASSIGNMENTS

The job descriptions on the next pages will help you overview the different tasks involved in producing plays. Do not be intimidated by all the positions. Read them over until you are familiar with them. If you don't have enough people to fill all the positions, you may combine jobs. Three examples of how the jobs may be divided are shown below and on the next page. **The important point is that everyone knows their role in the production and performs it!**

SMALL PRODUCTION:

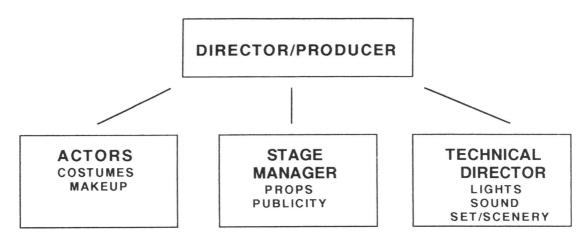

SMALL TO MEDIUM PRODUCTION:

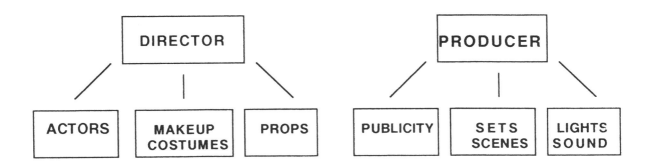

LARGER PRODUCTION:
Next page shows how jobs may be divided in a large production, with many people available to assist.

16

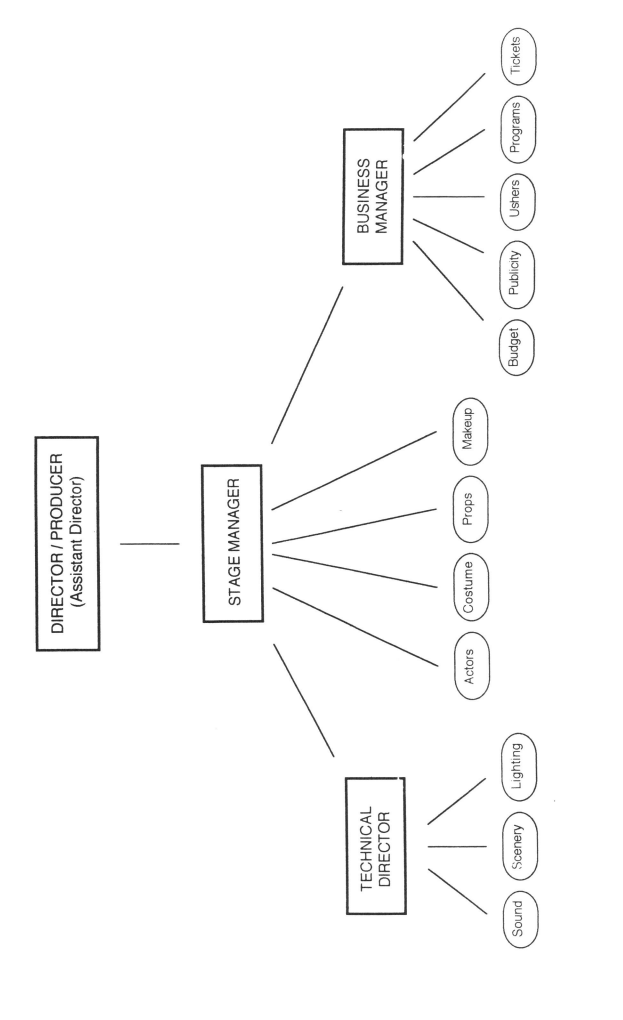

In professional theater, the Producer is responsible for the entire play including play selection, making the schedules and supervising publicity. All production crew, except the actors, report directly to the Producer. This frees the Director to put all his energies into directing the actors and the creative aspects of the play. Often the Director will be in charge of the cast and the Stage Manager will oversee the technical aspects such as lighting, sound, etc., of the production during rehearsals.

Regardless of how you divide the responsibilities, <u>someone</u> <u>must</u> know what each person is doing so that all the pieces of the production fit together and on time!

In the following pages you will see "boxes" placed around some job titles (see PRODUCER below). These are the head staff and any job titles listed below a "boxed" job title work under that staff person. This staff member is responsible to respond to any questions or problems that arise from those people working underneath him. **Taking problems to other staff members can cause problems and confusion!** If your staff member cannot solve the problem or answer a question, he should discuss it at a weekly production staff meeting.

PRODUCER

    – produces the entire play

    – selects the play

    – makes schedules, including monthly calendar with all dates of production scheduled (Director makes rehearsal schedule)

    – supervises publicity

    Everyone reports to the Producer, except the actors.

    (If no Producer is available, the Director assumes these responsibilities.)

DIRECTOR

- interprets the best possible way to present the play's message

- determines mood and image for the play

- oversees and manages the audition

- determines the actors for each character in the play

- directs and schedules rehearsals (see page 28)

- determines set design and floor plan for each scene

- discusses his ideas for set design with the Set Designer

- discusses his costume ideas with the Costume Designer

- discusses his makeup ideas with the Makeup person

- discusses lighting and sound requirements with the Technical Director

- blocks all scenes (shows the actors where and when to move on stage)

- directs the actors' facial and vocal expressions and movements

- usually sits close to stage to help actors in the blocking rehearsals, then moves toward the back to detect any flaws during the refining rehearsals

- encourages cast and crew

ASSISTANT DIRECTOR:

- assists Director with creative ideas

- helps block the actors (shows the actors where and when to move on stage)

- runs rehearsals if the Director cannot be there   19

STAGE MANAGER

- has complete charge of everything that happens on stage or backstage during dress rehearsals and performances

- makes sure all props are in place and working properly before rehearsals and performances

- must be organized and aware of what is happening on stage and backstage at all times

- uses script or prompt book to aid in cuing lights, sound, and prop changes backstage

- handles any backstage emergencies and keeps the performance running smoothly

ACTORS/ACTRESSES:

- present the play to the audience

- represent the characters in the play

- are at rehearsals *ON TIME*

- come to rehearsals with script lines memorized by appointed date

- are ready when the Director calls them to work on their scene

- wait quietly between scenes

- are under the direction of the Director during auditions and rehearsals, then Stage Manager assumes the direction during dress rehearsal and performances

- Are flexible! Blocking may change unexpectedly.

**Make sure all costumes fit
well in advance of the performance**

COSTUME DESIGNER:

– must understand costume designs chosen by the Director

– makes or locates all costumes for the play

– makes sure all costumes fit well in advance of the performance

– checks all costumes under stage lighting, from the middle of the auditorium, to make sure they look appropriate

– makes sure all costumes are cleaned and ironed before and after each performance, if needed

– labels all costumes with the actor's name and hangs them together ready for use during dress rehearsal and performances

21

MAKEUP PERSON:

- knows how the Director wishes the makeup to look on each character

- sets up makeup for dress rehearsal and performance

- teaches the actors or makeup crew how to apply the makeup

- checks the actors' makeup under stage lights for appropriate amount and effect

- cleans up the mess, making sure that brushes are clean, lids are on tight, and makeup stored properly after each use

PROMPTER:

- gives actors their lines if they have forgotten them

- makes changes to the master script or prompt book during rehearsals for the Director

(Prompter is needed only if desired by the Director. Prompter may be seated in the front row of audience or the Stage Manager may prompt from backstage.)

STAGE CREW:

- assists the stage manager backstage with scene changes

- arranges props on stage (or backstage to be ready for another scene)

- helps with costume changes, if needed.

TECHNICAL DIRECTOR

– gives estimates of the cost for the set, sound, and lighting to the business manager

– orders supplies to construct set

– schedules construction times with crews

– supervises the construction, painting, and/or obtaining of the set

– rents or obtains any special lights, recorded sounds, or other special effects needed for the production

– recruits people to run the lights, sound, etc.

– plans extra rehearsals with the technical crew to fix any trouble spots as needed

LIGHTING/SOUND CREW:

– operates the lights and sound effects

– is extremely focused (not easily distracted) and accurate (If a mistake is made in sound or light cues, it cannot be covered up. The audience will probably notice.)

– attends several rehearsals and dress rehearsals to learn timing

SET/SCENERY DESIGNER:

- understands set designs requested by the Director

- draws or makes models of scenes, if necessary

- decides placement, sizes, colors, and materials of sets

- makes, buys, borrows, or rents scenery to be used in the play (see page 58 for ideas)

BUDGET MANAGER

- manages all finances for the play

- keeps records of all expenses and income (if any) for the production

- oversees ticket sales

- collects all receipts for purchases, such as costumes, props, lighting, etc. made by production crews

PROGRAM DESIGNER:

- acknowledges **everyone** who helped in the production, no matter how small the job or time commitment in the program! Makes sure everyone is listed!

- makes sure everyone's name is correctly spelled

- includes acknowledgements of those who donated costumes, sets, or props in the program

- writes a short summary of the play so audience has some background information; may include a paragraph about each actor, previous credits, etc.

- designs and prints the programs

PUBLICITY MANAGER:

- informs the public of the performance date, time, and location of the play

- makes or buys advertising posters and posts them where the intended audience will see

- places ads or announcements in newspapers or on the radio (see page 58 for ideas of places to advertise)

- sends invitations, if appropriate, to intended audience

USHERS:

- dress attractively, smile, and are pleasant

- greet the people who come to watch the performance in a warm, friendly manner

- give the audience their programs

- direct the people to their seats

- make sure the theater is clean before and after performances

(Remember, ushers represent the entire group!)

MAKING A REHEARSAL SCHEDULE:

- consider how many weeks you have to prepare for the play
- consider the length and difficulty of the play
- consider the time availability of the cast
- decide how often to have rehearsals and their length
- fill in rehearsal schedule with date, time, location, purpose, and cast required (see below)

(Blank schedule sheet is available for your use on page 72)

Sample Rehearsal Schedule for "Visitor in Missionaryland"

Mon	April 20	7-8:30	Rm 129	Memorize Scene 1 Block Scene 1 Visitor & Missionary
Mon	April 27	7-8:30	Rm 129	Memorize Scene 2 Block Scene 2 Run through Scene 1 & 2 Visitor, Missionary, Seller, & crowd, if using
Mon	May 4	7-8:30	Rm 129	Memorize Scene 3 Block Scene 3 Run through Scenes 1,2,3 Entire cast
Mon	May 11	7-8:30	Rm 129	Run through entire play two times (three times if possible) Entire cast
Thur	May 14	7-8:30	Rm 129	Run through entire play (two to three times if possible) Entire cast
Mon	May 18	7-8:30	Rm 129	Run through entire play
Thur	May 21	7-8:30	Sanctuary	Run through Entire cast & production crews
Fri	May 22	7-9:30	Sanctuary	Dress Rehearsal Entire cast & production crews
Sat	May 23	7:00pm	Sanctuary	Performance
Sun	May 24	7:00pm	Sanctuary	Performance

(Be sure to consider how early the actors and crew should arrive before each performance to allow adequate time to prepare.)

27

HOW THE PUZZLE PIECES FIT TOGETHER
A Quick Overview

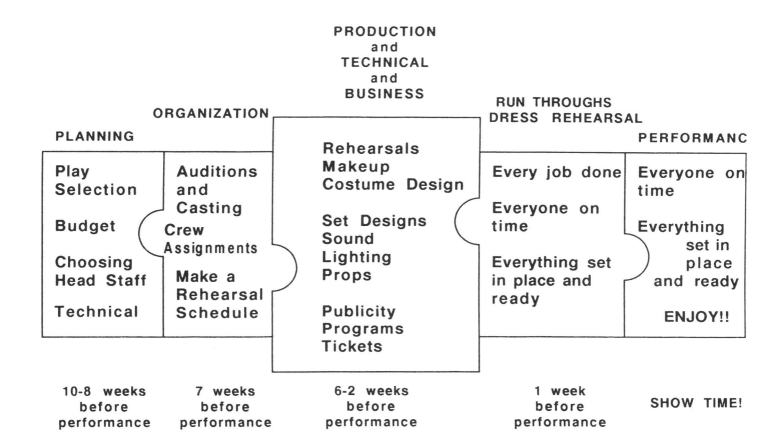

PLANNING	**ORGANIZATION**	**PRODUCTION and TECHNICAL and BUSINESS**	**RUN THROUGHS DRESS REHEARSAL**	**PERFORMANC**
Play Selection Budget Choosing Head Staff Technical	Auditions and Casting Crew Assignments Make a Rehearsal Schedule	Rehearsals Makeup Costume Design Set Designs Sound Lighting Props Publicity Programs Tickets	Every job done Everyone on time Everything set in place and ready	Everyone on time Everything set in place and ready ENJOY!!
10-8 weeks before performance	7 weeks before performance	6-2 weeks before performance	1 week before performance	SHOW TIME!

WARNING: There will be a time during the production when everything may feel out of control. You may be time-pressured and stressed even with prayer, good planning, and organization. If you look at the middle puzzle piece above, you will see why. Notice this is the busiest time in the production. Everyone is working hard to complete their tasks, nothing is completed yet and time is getting short. Everything is in a state of fluctuation and uncertainty. The pressure is on! Relax, don't panic! This is normal. Keep your communication going and pray without ceasing. Remember, **God is faithful!**

28

Production Schedule

8-10 weeks before performance:
(for skits in this book)

6-12 months for
major productions

1) Decide who the Director, Business Manager, and Technical Director will be
2) Choose play
3) Plan budget
4) Decide place, time, and date for auditions; send out and post announcements
5) Set dates and times of weekly staff meetings

WEEKS TO GO	COSTUMES	MAKEUP	PUBLICITY	SET SCENERY	LIGHTING	SOUND	PROPS	ACTORS
7 WEEKS	Sign-up crew	Sign-up crew	Sign-up crew	Sign-up crew	Sign-up crew	Sign-up crew	Sign-up crew	Audition
6 WEEKS	Plan with Director List needs	Plan with Director List needs	Plan where to advertise	Plan with Director List needs	Read script List needs	Read script List needs	Plan with Director List needs	Rehearsal
5 WEEKS	Take measure-ments of actors	Order Makeup	Create posters Place ads	Order materials	Find and/or make	Find and/or make	Find and/or make	Rehearsal
4 WEEKS	Make Find Fit	Try on actors under stage lights	Plan and design program	Paint Build	Find and/or make	Tape sounds if needed	Use temporary props if needed	Rehearsal
3 WEEKS	Make Find Fit	Make any adjustments Hairdos	Continue posting announce-ments	Paint Build	Find and/or make	Go over cues and finalize	All props Lay out plans for prop table	Rehearsal
2 WEEKS	Final Fit Check on stage	Hairdos finalized	Finalize program	Paint Build Set up on stage if possible	Find and/or make On stage if possible	Run with rehearsal	All props Lay out final plans	Rehearsal
1 WEEK	Ready	Train actors or makeup crew	Program printed and ready	Set up on stage	All lights in place	Run with rehearsal	Set in place	Run Throughs Dress Rehearsal
Dress Rehearsal Performance	On actors	On actors Hair done	Unsold tickets on hand to sell Ushers ready	Set up on stage Checked	Set cues Run for play	Set cues Run for play	Set in place Checked	Act! Act! Act!

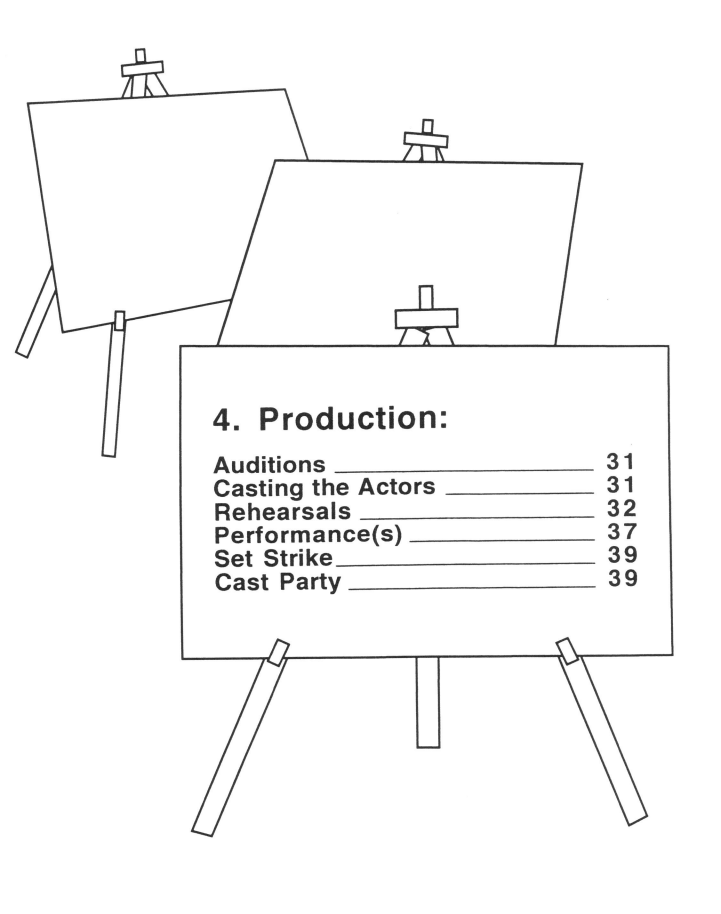

4. Production:

AUDITIONS:

– auditions are not a test, but a placement of the actors who best portray the characters according to the Director's vision of the play

– Director introduces himself and helps actors feel welcome and relaxed

– each actor fills out the Audition Questionnaire (see page 70)

– to relax before reading, the actor may walk around a bit, shake out his arms and hands, and take deep breaths

– actors read part of the skit aloud or come prepared with a monologue (song if auditioning for a Musical)

– actors can read in pairs to save time and help each other relax

– Director takes notes during the audition and compares the strengths of the actors to the characters he envisions for the play

– Director thanks everyone for auditioning and either assigns parts to actors at the end of the audition or informs them at a later time

CASTING THE ACTORS:

– Director considers the actor's voice, poise, and how well the actor reads the part

– Director decides which actor has the physical traits to portray the characters in the play (A six foot male, acting as a toddler with a five foot father would not be believable unless the script had a specific purpose for it).

– those not chosen as characters in the play may help in other areas of the production

REHEARSALS:

1) First Rehearsal:

- introduce all cast and production crews

- Director makes everyone feel confident and expresses the enjoyment of putting on a play

- Director hands out rehearsal schedules to each person in the production

- Director describes how the play will be expressed and any additional changes to the script

- Director reads through the play with entire cast and production crew

- Director explains everyone's role in the production

- Director answers any questions and makes sure actors understand what action and/or feelings happen in each scene

- each actor takes notes of his characterization, diction, and tempo from the Director's instructions

- take measurements for any costumes (if needed) by the first or second rehearsal

- props, sets, and costumes should be started at the beginning of production and be completely ready well in advance of dress rehearsal

2) Blocking Rehearsals:
(Plan at least one rehearsal for each scene of the play)

– practice where the play will be performed, if possible; otherwise practice in a place with similar size. Set up and use the area as you would your real stage (see pages 44 and 45)

– have only those actors involved in a certain scene attend the appropriate rehearsal (if someone is needed for only part of the rehearsal have them come late or dismiss them early)

– Director explains when, where, or how the actors will move during a scene.
   1) Actors should not cross between the actor who is speaking and the audience. Always cross behind the speaking actor when possible.
   2) Makes sure that actors do not turn their backs to the audience unless it has a direct purpose. (Usually the script will indicate this if needed.)

– blocking rehearsals are usually slow, but very important

– actors practice movements or action on stage until the movements feel natural

– practice entrances and exits for each scene so they are smooth and no one walks into each other

– watch for and correct any nervous habits of the actors such as swaying, shifting feet, fidgeting, playing with hair, etc.

– avoid interpretation of lines; too much detail will confuse the actor--just practice basic movements (interpretation is done during Refining Rehearsals on next page)

– correct any major problems: it is harder to relearn something than it is to learn it right the first time

– all gestures should have a purpose; use BIG gestures

– use different actions to break up long speeches (two people talking without any action is boring to the audience)

- walk through Scene 1, directing where and when to move on stage

- after blocking of Scene 1 is worked out, go on to Scene 2

- run through Scene 1 and Scene 2 together for continuity

- block Scene 3, then run through 1 and 2 again with 3

3) Refining Rehearsals:
(One to three depending on length and difficulty of play and actors' abilities)

- work on places in any scene that are still not flowing smoothly or in which actors lack confidence

- work through <u>each</u> scene to add more facial expressions and more detailed body movement, helping to create feeling and emotion in the scenes.

- all props must be in place by these rehearsals, sooner if possible

4) Technical Rehearsals:
(Usually one or as many as needed)

- Technical rehearsals are usually long, but extremely important. They help develop the quickest and smoothest way to change scenes, work out lighting, and check sound problems.

- run through the play one scene at a time to make sure all cues for lighting, sound, and scene changes are correct and changes have been made in the prompt book (This rehearsal is usually done without actors. The Director or Stage Manager reads through the script with the Technical Crew.)

5) Run-through Rehearsals:
(Usually two to three times)

- all costumes are ready, but not worn until Dress Rehearsal

- all props are in place on stage

- all sets are ready backstage and Scene 1 is set up and ready

- Master Script or Prompt Book is current and easy to read

- sound effects are cued up (ready)

- lighting is in place and ready when needed

- final assignment of backstage crew for scene changes or backstage sound effects

- **NO STOPPING in a Run-through--practice it straight through! (God Bless! This is almost impossible.)**

- after Run-through, Director makes any *slight* changes or improvements

- time the play to see if it is running on schedule

- if you plan to video the play, have the video person attend so he knows where and when actors enter and exit, and where to shoot close-ups, etc.

6) Dress Rehearsal:
(One day before the performance)

- Stage Manager is in charge of the entire show

- Stage Manager and backstage crew in place and ready for scene changes and backstage sound effects

- Director encourages cast and crew to give them confidence

- all actors in full costume and makeup

- all props for Scene 1 in place on stage

- offstage props/scenery are all set and ready backstage

- sound person knows all cues, is ready and in place

- sound effects are cued and ready at correct volume

- lighting person is ready and in place

- lighting is ready and any special lighting is positioned properly

- practice curtain call (when and how to bow together)

- all costumes are labeled with actors' names and hung together when dress rehearsal is done

- any costume pressing must be done before performance

- straight run through; Director makes and discusses final notes with cast and crews

PERFORMANCE(S):

- Director and/or Stage Manager arrive at least two hours before performance to make sure everything is in place

- Actors arrive at least one hour before performance. You must allow sufficient time, *without rushing,* for everyone to get into costume, apply makeup, and for any last minute cast meetings.

- all production crews arrive at least one hour early

- Director encourages cast and crew to give them confidence

- full costumes on

- makeup applied

- Stage Manager is in charge, he runs the entire show

- Stage Crew is in place and ready to do any scene changes

- all props for Scene 1 in place on stage

- offstage props ready backstage

- all sets in place on stage or ready backstage

- sound effects are cued and ready at correct volume

- lighting is ready and any special lighting is positioned properly

- Stage Manager and Stage Crew in place and ready

- ushers ready with programs

- always treat the audience with respect

— no one shc .d appear on stage or in front of the curtain after the auditorium is open to the audience

— Be very quiet backstage! The audience should not hear anything that distracts them from the show.

— The audience should not see anyone backstage as this distracts from the show. Remember, during the performance, if you can see the audience, they can see you! Stay out of sight!

— All actors and stage crews backstage stay in position during each scene. If actors forget part of the script, the scene may end early. Don't assume scene timing! Be ready!

— Relax and have fun! You've worked hard and you're ready!

Everyone encourages each other to relieve nerves!

Everyone takes a deep breath, relax, and have fun!

After the performance, when people compliment your performance say, "Thank you". Even if you missed some cues, don't tell them the mistakes you made. This would make them feel awkward. Instead, be gracious and say, "I'm glad you enjoyed it!" Then thank them for coming.

SET STRIKE:

        – <u>Everyone</u> puts away all production props, sets, costumes, and cleans up entire theater area (including stage, backstage, and audience area).

        – make sure all costumes are clean before they are stored or returned

        – have one person responsible for immediately returning all borrowed or rented items

        – make sure that makeup containers are clean, lids are on tight and stored properly for future productions

CAST PARTY:

        – usually scheduled the following week

        – Discuss how well the production was performed--was it a success?

        – If it was not a success, what could you do differently on your next production to improve the performance? This discussion is very important as it teaches you more than any book ever will.

        – share compliments given by audience to cast

        – eat snacks and relax

        – watch video, if taken

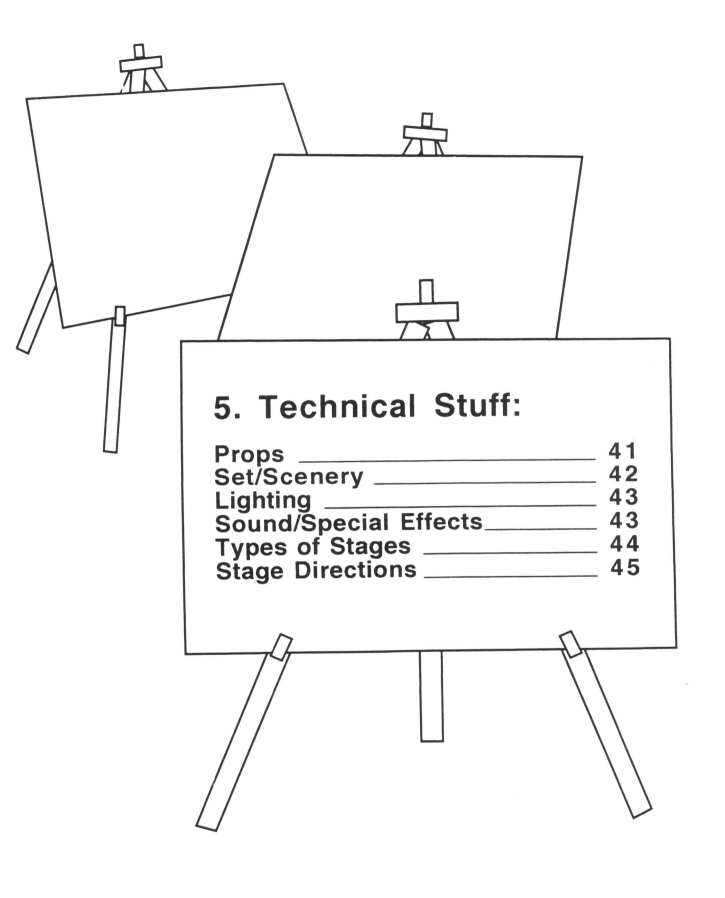

5. Technical Stuff:

PROPS:

- anything used by an actor during the play is called a prop (short for property)

- make sure all props work properly and are durable enough to last through rehearsals and performances

- arrange all props in an orderly fashion on a table backstage; if all props are put in one designated area it is easier to locate them for each scene (see example of a Prop Table below)

- mark props with their corresponding scene numbers (if possible)

- if props are dangerous (swords, spears, etc.), store in a safe place

- **Do not play with any props. They can be damaged or damage you!**

Prop Table Example From "Visitor In Missionaryland"

Stage Door

SET/SCENERY:

- lets the audience know where a scene occurs, what room of the house, season of the year, part of the country, time of day, etc.

- gives an illusion of a place; for example, an office desk, chair, and file cabinet is enough to suggest an office

- tells the audience the social status of the characters

- creates the feeling or mood of play

- must be practical, durable, and usually portable enough to be moved on and off the stage

- does not have to be totally realistic, solid, or even complete

- must be the correct size in proportion to actors

- must be located in the right position to make the scene effective, but not block the action on stage

- not used for the entire play should be clearly marked with scene number

Many good books are available at the library to help you design and build any kind of set. (See Resource Chapter)

LIGHTING:

- helps set the mood of a scene (example: using blue light can give the illusion of dusk, night, or a dream)

- helps indicate the time of a scene (dusk, night, etc.)

- turning the lights "on" or "off" suggests beginning and ending of scenes for the audience, or the passing of a day

- enter lighting cues into the prompt book or master script

SOUND/SPECIAL EFFECTS:

- consist of live sound on stage, live sound backstage, or recorded sounds (examples: phone ringing, doorbell, thunder, squealing tires)

- help set the mood for what is happening on stage (example: suspenseful music played at intense time in the play)

- can be simple or complicated

- can be rented or purchased on tape

- music may be used before the performance, during a scene, and during intermission for mood and/or enjoyment

- the sound level must be balanced with the actors' voice levels so it is realistic to the scene

- need to be loud enough to be heard by the audience

- volume and length of each sound effect must be written carefully in master script or prompt book

- leave a few seconds' space between each effect, if recorded

- decide placement of any sound equipment--such as microphones--on or around stage area

- must be used in several rehearsals; allows practice for actors and technicians to adjust timing and correct failed effects

43

TYPES OF STAGES:

Three basic types:

1) Proscenium stage is the most common stage. The stage is directly in front of the audience.

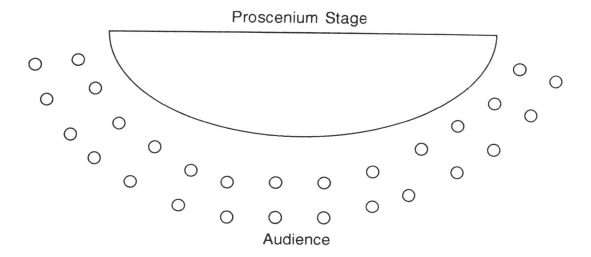

2) The audience sits around three sides of the Thrust stage; which also extends out into the audience area. Scenery is placed at the back of the stage, so it doesn't block the view from the audience.

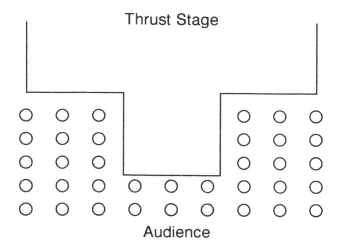

3) The audience completely surrounds the Arena stage, also called "Theater in the Round". Scenery must be three dimensional and sized so as not to block the view of action on stage from anywhere in the audience.

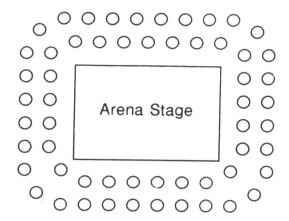

STAGE DIRECTIONS:

The Director uses stage directions during blocking rehearsals to tell the actors where to move on the stage. Stage directions are always given from the actor's point of view on stage. Originally, theaters were higher at the back of the stage and lower in the front so the audience could see all the action on stage. Hence, this gives one an understanding of the terms upstage and downstage. If the directions are too confusing or there is no time to learn them, you may use simpler terms such as "move to front right stage" or "move to center back stage". Whatever you decide, **always** use terms viewed from the **Actor's left or right, not** the Director's.

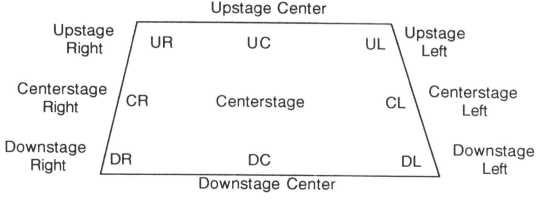

AUDIENCE

6. Makeup/Costumes:

BASIC MAKEUP:

Everyone will need some makeup. If stage lights are used, they tend to wash out normal skin colors. Also, normal facial features seem indistinct to the audience. The actor's hair as well as his face, is included when doing makeup.

FOUNDATION:

The two basic kinds of foundation makeup are grease paint and pancake. The two foundations can be used together, but it is easier to use one or the other. Grease paint usually comes in tubes or sticks and has a creamy base. It is spread directly on the face with your fingers or a sponge. If you use grease paint, you will need powder to "set" the makeup or it may smear or shine. You may match the powder to the foundation colors, but translucent or neutral shades are more easily reused for another play. To apply powder, with brush or dab on with a powder puff. Be sure to wipe off excess powder.

Pancake makeup is a dry or nearly dry solid mixed with water and applied to the skin with a wet sponge. If you use pancake foundation, you will need porous sponges (natural sponges are ideal). (Don't use the makeup wedges that standard non-stage makeup requires.)

You must remove all makeup after the show. To remove grease paint, use cold cream or makeup remover. Pancake foundation is easily removed with cold cream or soap and water.

Makeup List:

- face cream

- foundation (pancake or grease)

- powder

- makeup necessary for contouring, highlighting and special effects

- blush

- eye shadow

- eye liner

- mascara

- eyebrow pencils of several shades

- powder puff

- makeup brushes in several sizes (one each for blush and eye shadow)

- natural sponges

- lip brushes or Q-tips

- items for clean up:

    - cold cream

    - washcloths

    - makeup remover

    - eye makeup remover

APPLICATION STEPS:

1) Cleanse your face and neck thoroughly or your makeup will not go on evenly and your face will look like a *dirty mess*.

2) Wear old clothes or a towel around your neck. **Don't wear your costume until makeup is complete--trust me on this one!**

3) Apply face cream, if desired to help foundation go on smoothly and allow easier removal of makeup after the performance.

4) Have sponges ready to apply either grease or pancake foundation.

5) Read the directions on the container before applying any makeup.

6) Choose a foundation color--usually one to two shades darker than your skin color.

7) Apply foundation to your face, including areas over the eyes, ears, and neck that will show above your costume. Smooth out any streaks or lumps. You want to cover your face, but not look like you are wearing a mask.

   - To apply grease paint, put small dots all over your face and spread with your fingers until smooth and even.

   - To apply cake foundation, dip the sponge in water and then squeeze it out. It should be moist, but not dripping. Rub sponge in cake and then on your face. You may have to moisten the sponge occasionally. If the foundation flakes, the sponge is too dry. If it is streaky or has run marks, the sponge is too wet.

8) Check foundation color under stage lighting. If the color is too dark or light, clean it off and try another color.

9) Apply blush color to cheeks. Make sure the blush tone doesn't clash with the foundation color. Apply along and below the cheekbone (see example below). Check under stage lights. Add more blush color gradually, if needed. It is easier to put more on than to take some off. Blend well with your fingers or brush.

CHEEKS

MALE

- to apply cheek color draw an imaginary line from center of pupil down face

- blush should stay on the outside of that line

- apply brown shade of blush using this line in horizontal strokes to bottom half of ear <u>not</u> along the cheekbone

- blend

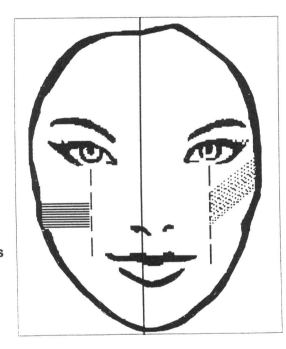

FEMALE

- to apply cheek color draw an imaginary line from center of pupil down face

- blush should stay on the outside of that line

- apply blush from this line at the apple (center) of the cheek angled up toward hair above the ear

- blend

50

10) Contouring helps define your face so it will not look flat from the audience. Choose a darker color of foundation or matte bronzing powder, to contour and add depth to the nose, jaw line, chin, and temple areas (see example below).

CONTOUR

MALE

- small dabs of brown contour at temples

- blended lines along jaw line

- blended lines on sides of nose

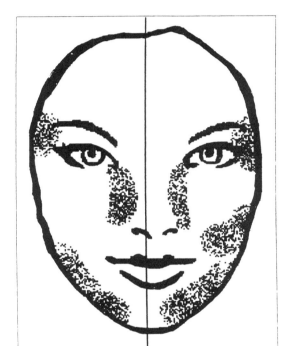

FEMALE

- small dabs of brown contour at temples

- blended lines along jaw line

- blended lines on sides of nose

- contour under cheek bones

11) If using grease paint, use face powder to set makeup now. Dip the puff into the powder and pat it onto the entire face with your eyes closed. You may need help with this step. Brush off the excess powder so no powder grains are visible. Do not rub off. Rubbing will take the makeup off and you will have to start over.

12) Both men and women, put on eye shadow as shown in example. Women add additional color as needed.

BEFORE   **AFTER**

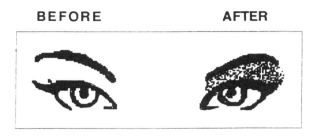

cover entire eye area with light beige

13) Use eye liner to emphasize the eyes or they will not be seen by the audience. When using a makeup pencil hold it perpendicular to your face. This will help keep the lines clear and sharp. Draw a very thin line above the upper eyelashes and just below the bottom eyelashes. Have actor close eyes to apply liner to upper lids; look upwards and away to apply to the lower lid. Dark haired, dark skinned actors use black eye liner pencil. Blonde haired, light skinned actors use dark brown eye liner.

BEFORE   **AFTER**

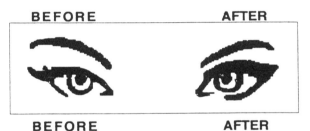

line upper lash 3/4 to outside line lower lash 1/2 way to outside
apply mascara

BEFORE   **AFTER**

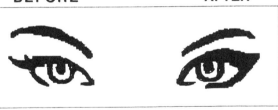

for close set eyes only line eyes 1/2 way on the top

BEFORE   **AFTER**

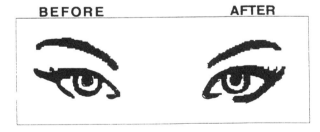

for deep set eyes don't line the top at all

52

14) If you need to darken and define eyebrows, use eyebrow pencils. Use them lightly with a series of very short, light, feathery strokes. Follow the natural hairline of the eyebrow unless you are creating a certain look.

15) Apply lip liner to give the lips definition. (see example below).

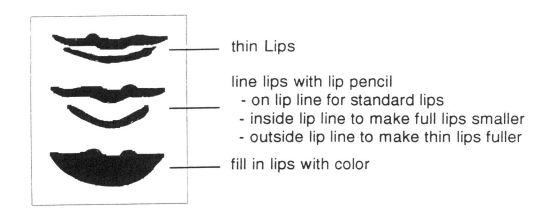

thin Lips

line lips with lip pencil
 - on lip line for standard lips
 - inside lip line to make full lips smaller
 - outside lip line to make thin lips fuller

fill in lips with color

16) Apply lipstick. For male actors use a lipstick that is natural or has brown tones. Do not use any red tone lipsticks for the guys. Ben Nye brand "Natural" lip color is a good choice.

17) Check makeup one final time <u>under stage lighting</u>, preferably from the middle of the theater (make sure actors' faces are visible and not flat).

18) Clean up your makeup mess and put on your costume

Good theatrical makeup companies are: Ben Nye, Bob Kelly, and Mehron (see Resource Chapter)

In general, the performers can do their own makeup, or you can assign someone to do it for them. In a large production, you may want a makeup crew. This crew runs in an assembly line fashion--each person is trained to do one makeup step. This is more time efficient and the makeup will look more uniform.

Many good books for special effects such as aging are available in the public library. (see Resource Chapter)

HAIR:

Choose hair styles that help define the character to the audience. There are many kinds of liquids, sprays, and temporary hair colorings to choose from on the market. Whichever you choose, make sure you cover all the hair, not just the outside layer.

Make sure the hair is securely in place so it does not distract the actor or the audience by falling or slipping during the performance. There are many styling products to choose from. Use ones that state "Maximum Hold", but make sure before the performance that they work.

Hair Items List:

- hair spray (hair spray and spray on hair color can be very toxic to breathe, spray in well ventilated area if possible)
- temporary hair coloring (if needed)
- bobby pins
- rubber bands
- rubber gloves (if using spray on hair color)
- comb and hairbrush (actors should bring own)
- curling irons and/or hot curlers

COSTUMES:

- visually convey information about the character to the audience

- let the audience know the age, wealth, and social position

- indicate the time period in which the character lives

- indicate the type of job the character has in the play

- let the audience know the basic nature and personality of the character

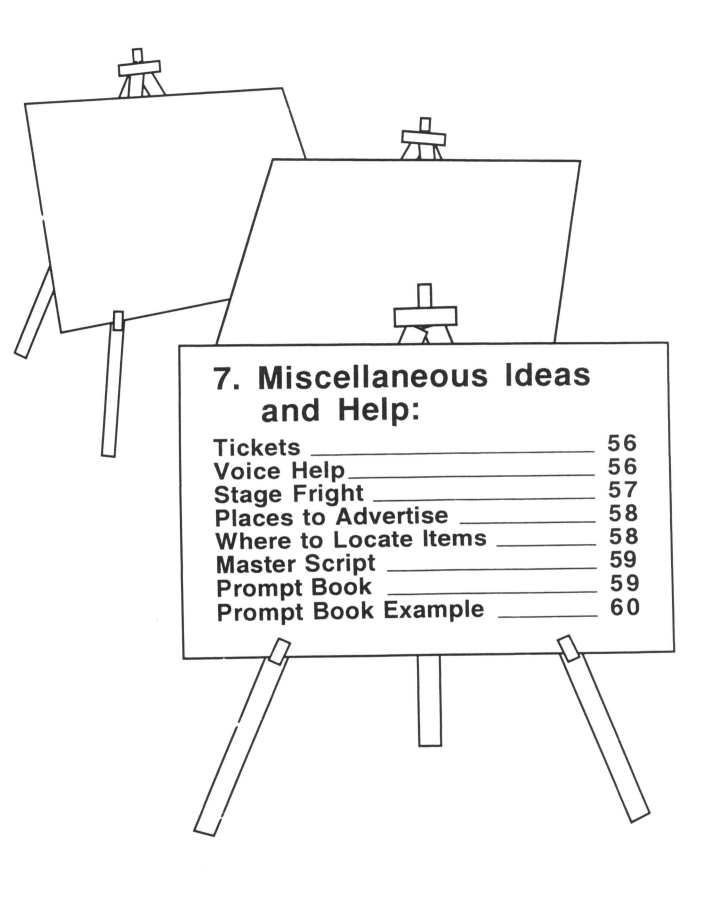

7. Miscellaneous Ideas and Help:

TICKETS:

- can be used regardless of whether you charge admission or not (this is a good way to keep track of attendance and help make sure there is enough seating)

- may be purchased at office supply stores

- can be designed by you and then printed

VOICE HELP:

- speak *slowly and pronounce* each word with enough volume for the audience to hear the play's message

- don't rush your lines

- speeding up or slowing down words or phrases, as well as pitching your voice higher or lower, will help convey a certain meaning or clarify the mood of the play to the audience

- speaking faster will increase tension and create a higher vocal pitch

- the volume of your voice must be loud enough to be heard by the audience but not forced, which causes strained vocal cords

- Use projection to direct your volume to the back of the theater. Pretend the actor you are talking to on stage is at the farthest point away in the theater. Use your diaphragm to push the air out of your lungs.

- be prepared to stop speaking or "hold" for an audience laugh or applause during the performance

STAGE FRIGHT:

Stage fright is usually caused by the desire to do a good job. We don't want to let ourselves or others down. This is only natural. Don't panic! If you have practiced your part and know your lines, you will be fine. Besides many "mistakes" are not even noticed by the audience. Some mistakes actually improve the play! (Example: see middle of page 94 in the Missionary skit. These lines were added to the skit when the missionary tripped the visitor while walking. They ad-libbed and no one ever knew.)

- An actor may forget the exact words of a line during a rehearsal. Unless it would lose the meaning, an actor may say the lines in his own words.

- If you are nervous or tense, walk around a little. Shake out your arms. Take a deep breath and exhale slowly.

- Remember, waiting for the play to begin is usually more stressful than the actual performance.

PLACES TO ADVERTISE:

- newspaper (Approximately one month before performance)

- radio and TV stations (Check with your local stations for their deadline)

(call the above places about press releases, too)

- free community bulletin boards

- store windows

- church bulletins (including churches other than your own)

- various support groups

- senior and community centers

- boys and girls clubs

WHERE TO LOCATE ITEMS: (COSTUMES, PROPS, LIGHTING, ETC.)

- thrift stores/secondhand stores

- community theater in your area (borrow or rent)

- high school theaters (borrow or rent)

- friends

- family

- businesses

People are usually very happy to help out by donating or lending items. Make sure the donors are given credit in the program and that anything borrowed is returned in good condition promptly after the performance.

The public library has many excellent books containing great ideas and information about set design, makeup, costumes, acting, plays, and any other aspect you will ever need. Check a few books out and enjoy!

58

MASTER SCRIPT:

> – a copy of the script where the Director writes **all** the cues for actors, lighting, sound, etc.

> – use a different color for each type of cue (blue for actor, red for sound, green for lighting, and so on)

> – each production head either receives a copy of the master script and highlights the cues that pertain to his job, or copies the cues from the master script into his own script and highlights the cues

Prompt Book

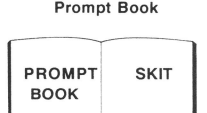

PROMPT BOOK:

> – paste one page of script on right side of notebook; on the left side write down actors' movements, lighting, and sound cues (see example of prompt book on next page)

> – use a different color pen for each different cue (blue for actor, red for sound, green for lighting, etc.)

(If you do not use a prompt book, but prefer to place all notes within the script, it is still a good idea to highlight all cues as specified above.)

"VISITOR IN MISSIONARYLAND" PROMPT BOOK EXAMPLE

BLOCKING -
(*Missionary pays Seller and hands tract to him.*
Missionary and Visitor walk triumphantly towards home.
Seller looks at tract and then throws it away.

Missionary pays Seller and hands tract to him.
Missionary and Visitor walk triumphantly towards home.
Seller looks at tract and then throws it away.

LIGHTS -
(*Lights out or exit back around to hut scene*)
Lights off.

······································

SCENE THREE

SETTING -
Setting: Missionary hut (see scene one)

LIGHTS -
          (*Lights On*)
Missionary hut.
Lights on.

BLOCKING -
(*Back home, Visitor is putting away food in or on crate in corner*)

Visitor: Oh! . . .(*jumping back from the crate*) What's that?

Missionary: Oh, dear! I should have warned you . . . we tend to have a
             bit of a bug problem here. Ants in the sugar, cockroaches
             and spiders most everywhere. Don't worry, you'll get used
             to their surprises.

Missionary and Visitor walk into hut. Visitor is carrying
the food and walks over to crate to put away.
Visitor jumps back away from crate.

          (*Visitor looks toward audience with extremely dubious expression and mouths*
          "I don't think so," as she shakes her head)

Visitor looks towards audience with an extremely dubious
expression and mouths "I don't think so" as she shakes her head.

Missionary: Well, it's siesta time. (*Missionary exits*)

Missionary exits stage right.

Visitor: (*Visitor sits on cot with diary.*) I am tired and it is so....
             (*jumps up quickly to check for bugs.* With relief she reseats
             herself) hot!

Visitor walks to cot with diary and starts to sit down.
Jumps back up looking for bugs.

BLOCKING -
          (*Visitor lies down to nap and is molested by mosquitoes. Swats the air, finally*
          visitor triumphs over bug and sleeps 10 seconds.)

SOUND -
          ("*Flight of the Bumble Bee* "is a great sound effect or record buzzing noises.)
          (*Missionary enters with dinner on a tray.*)

Visitor lies down to nap and is molested by mosquitoes.
Swats the air.
Music "Flight of the Bumble Bee" or sound effect of
buzzing mosquito.

BLOCKING -
Missionary: Well, here's dinner. Since it's your first night here I thought
             you'd enjoy a native delicacy called Balut.
             (*Sets tray on the table.*)

Finally triumphs over bug and sleeps for 10 seconds. Starts to get up.
Missionary enters with dinner on a tray.
Missionary sets tray on table.

Visitor: M-m-m. Sounds great! (*Enthusiastically*) What is it?!

Missionary: Oh, it's a duck egg that was buried so the baby wasn't
             able to hatch. (*Visitor looks aghast.*) It's quite tasty.

Visitor turns to audience and looks aghast

60

61

Glossary

Glossary

actors - the people who portray the characters in a play

ad-lib - actors make up dialogue as they go if they can't remember their lines

arena stage - a theater in which the audience surrounds the entire stage

audience - the people who come to watch the performance

auditions - a trial demonstration for the actor who attempts to obtain a part in a play

backstage - the area behind the performing space, including the wings and the dressing rooms, that the audience cannot see

blocking - where and when the actors move on stage

budget manager - the person responsible for the finances and any part of the production. May also be in charge of publicity and ushers.

cast - the actors in the play

casting - choosing the actors for each character in the play

characters - the people in a play portrayed by the actors

comedy - a type of play that uses humor in the script

contouring - using a dark powder or cream makeup to help define the actor's face so it doesn't look flat from the audience's perspective

costumes - what the actors wear in the play to portray their characters

costume designer - the person who creates and/or obtains the costumes for the cast

cue - an action or line in the script that signals another actor to come on stage or begin speaking; also could be a change in lighting or sound effect

curtain call - the reappearance of the cast on stage during applause to bow after the play is over

diction - how words are pronounced, phrased, or enunciated

63

Glossary (continued)

director - the person responsible for interpreting the play, choosing and directing the actors, and managing the rehearsals

entrance - the first entry of the actor in the scene

exit - the departure of the actor from the stage

foundation - facial and neck makeup used to darken the actor's complexion so it can be seen clearly by the audience

gel - a colored medium placed in front of a light lens that changes the color of the light

gesture - movement of any part of the body to help thought or emphasize feeling

grease paint - is a type of foundation that comes in tubes, has a creamy base, and is spread directly on the face by sponge or fingers

lighting - use of special lights to create moods or scenes

lines - the dialogue of the play

live sound - any sound used in a production that is not recorded but produced by someone backstage or on stage

mood - the feeling the audience receives from all aspects of the production such as lighting, sound, costumes, etc.

musical - a play where the actors sing, and/or dance, or music is included

offstage - see backstage definition

performance - the putting on of the play before an audience

procure - to obtain something needed in the production

producer - person responsible for the entire play and supervises all crews

production - the act of putting on the entire play

Glossary (continued)

production crew - those people who help put on a play other than actors and director

program - a sheet or sheets with an overview of the play, a list of scenes, and a list of everyone involved in the production, including credits to those who have donated time, items, or money

projecting - to direct the actor's voice outward in order to be heard by the entire audience

prompt book - the script with all blocking and cues written into it, such as lighting, sound, etc.; each cue is usually highlighted with a different color

prompter - the person who gives the actor a forgotten line from offstage

proscenium stage - a theater in which the audience is seated directly in front of the stage

props - every article on stage except the scenery, usually easily movable

recorded sound - any sound on tape or other medium that is used in a play

rehearsal - the practice and repetition of a play by the actors, guided by the director, to prepare for a performance

rehearsal schedule - a plan list that includes time, date, people required, and place to meet in order to practice the play

scenery - see set/setting (examples: tables, chairs, backdrops, stairs, door frame and door, etc.)

script - a copy of the entire play

set/setting - the scenery that creates the environment or background for the entire play

set designer - person responsible for creating the set/scenery

set strike - removing all production props, sets, and costumes from the stage and cleaning up entire theater area

sound effects - imitative sounds produced artificially such as doorbells, telephone, etc. that help create the mood of the scene

65

Glossary (continued)

special effects - visual, lighting, or sound effects such as thunder or explosions that help create the mood of the scene

stage directions - directions from the actor's point of view given by the director that tell the actor where to move on stage

stage etiquette - the manners of the actors and entire production crews towards the audience, before, during, and after performances

stage manager - the person responsible for running the dress rehearsal and entire performance from beginning to end

technical director - the person who is in charge of the non-acting elements of the production (examples: lights, sound, etc.)

tempo - speed of speech or actions

thrust stage - a stage that extends out into the auditorium

tragedy - drama centered on unhappy events or powerful struggles

ushers - persons who pass out the programs, greet, and seat the audience

voice - how an actor makes his voice sound while playing a character (high or low pitch, slow, drawl, hyper, etc.)

volume - loudness of voice or sound effects

Reproducible Sheets:

DRAMA PRODUCTION BUDGET - POSSIBLE BUDGET ITEMS

INCOME

DONATIONS	TICKET SALES
Church	
Individuals	
Support Groups	

EXPENSES

ADVERTISING	COSTUMES	MAKEUP	MISC	PROPS	SET/SCENERY	SCRIPT
Posters	Material	Foundation	Programs	Thrift Store	Lumber	Rights to Play
Invitations	Thrift Store	Brushes	Copies	Rented	Paint	Copies (if allowed)
Newspaper	Rented	Sponges	Lighting	Lumber	Hardware	Royalties
Radio			Tickets	Paint	Carpeting	

SAMPLE DRAMA PRODUCTION BUDGET

INCOME

DONATIONS	TICKET SALES
Sally Jones $10.00	Pre-sales $125.00
Church budget $75.00	
Total $85.00	Total $125.00

EXPENSES

ADVERTISING	COSTUMES	MAKEUP	MISC	PROPS	SET/SCENERY	SCRIPT
Poster paper $10.00	Fabric $25.00	Foundation $10.00	Program printing $15.00	Crates deposit $5.00	Lumber $20.00	Copies $4.00
P-I Newspaper ad $17.00	Thread $2.50	Hair coloring $6.25	Lights rental $20.00	Bag of oranges $4.00		
Total $27.00	Total $27.50	Total $16.25	Total $35.00	Total $9.00	Total $20.00	Total $4.00

DRAMA PRODUCTION BUDGET

INCOME		EXPENSES							
DONATIONS	TICKET SALES	ADVERTISING	COSTUMES	MAKEUP	MISC	PROPS	SET/SCENERY	SCRIPT

Audition Questionnaire

Name: _____

Age: _____   Sex: _____   Home Phone: _____
                                   Work Phone: _____

Role: _____Large _____ Medium _____ Small

Previous Experience: _____None   _____ Beginner
                     _____Intermediate   _____ Experienced

If previous experience list here: _____

_____

_____

_____

Sing?   _____Yes _____No

Dance?   _____Yes _____No

Play Instrument?   _____Yes _____No

        List: _____

Any other skills that might be used in production?

        Calligraphy   _____ Yes _____ No
        Sewing   _____ Yes _____ No
        Writing   _____ Yes _____ No
        Sound   _____ Yes _____ No
        Other   _____

Nights available to rehearse?
_____ Mon _____Tues_____ Wed _____Thur _____ Fri _____Sat_____ Sun

Hours available? _____ am_____pm

Please return to:

CREW SIGN-UP SHEET

CREW TITLE: _____

Name	JOB	PHONE #

Rehearsal Schedule

Day: _____ Date: _____ Time: _____ Location: _____

Purpose: _____

Cast to attend: _____

Day: _____ Date: _____ Time: _____ Location: _____

Purpose: _____

Cast to Attend: _____

Day: _____ Date: _____ Time: _____ Location: _____

Purpose: _____

Cast to Attend: _____

Day: _____ Date: _____ Time: _____ Location: _____

Purpose: _____

Cast to Attend: _____

Day: _____ Date: _____ Time: _____ Location: _____

Purpose: _____

Cast to Attend: _____

Day: _____ Date: _____ Time: _____ Location: _____

Purpose: _____

Cast to Attend: _____

Day: _____ Date: _____ Time: _____ Location: _____

Purpose: _____

Cast to Attend: _____

PRODUCTION MATERIALS FOR PROP CREW SAMPLE

ITEM	DESCRIPTION	SOURCE	COST IF APPLICABLE	IN	RETURN
Table & 3 chairs	Dark wood	Ed Jones 555-1212	Donated use of	4/20/95	5/25/95
Table 8' long for Seller's booth	Convention table 8' long wood	Brown's Engineering 555-2255	Donated use of	4/27/95	5/25/95
Box of Oranges	40 lb Box	Tony's Grocery 555-2133	$4.00	4/27/95	- - - - -
Stack of Bibles	10 Bibles black covers	Church Library	Donated use of	4/27/95	5/24/95
Cot	Army cot	Sal's Army Surplus 555-4575	Donated use of for performance only	5/23/95	5/25/95

PRODUCTION MATERIALS FOR _____

ITEM	DESCRIPTION	SOURCE	COST IF APPLICABLE	IN	RETURN

Dress Rehearsal/Performance Checklists
(Use the blank spaces between job titles to add your own list)

Stage Manager Checklist:

___ **props are ready**
    ___ all props for Scene 1 in place on stage and working
    ___ all other stage props ready backstage, in place, or on the prop table and working

___ **sets**
    ___ Scene 1 in place on stage and secure
    ___ other scene sets ready backstage

___ **costumes**
    ___ cleaned and ironed
    ___ labeled with actor's name
    ___ hung ready to wear in groups, according to appropriate scene

___ **makeup set out and ready to apply**
    ___ face cream
    ___ foundation
    ___ powder
    ___ eye shadow
    ___ eye liner
    ___ mascara
    ___ blush
    ___ eyebrow pencils
    ___ makeup for contouring, highlighting, and special effects
    ___ powder puff
    ___ makeup brushes
        ___ blush
        ___ contour (if using powder)
        ___ eye shadow
    ___ sponges for foundation
    ___ lip brushes for applying lip color (Q-tips may be used)
    ___ items for clean up:
        ___ cold cream
        ___ washcloths
        ___ makeup remover
        ___ eye makeup remover
        ___ water
        ___ towel

Dress Rehearsal/Performance Checklists

Actor Checklist:

___ makeup applied
___ hair done
___ full costume on

Technical Director Checklist:

___ sound effects are:
    ___ working
    ___ cued up (ready)
___ sound volumes are at the correct volume level
___ lighting
    ___ in place
    ___ working

Business Manager Checklist:

___ ushers in place with programs
___ theater is clean
___ seating is ready
___ ticket takers ready with tickets
___ cash box ready with appropriate change

Director Checklist:

___ encourages actors
___ oversees preparation of other staff, help where needed
___ makes any last minute reminders to actors
___ leads prayer before performance

Budget Checklist

The following items are to be considered when beginning a play.

<u>**Expenses**</u>   <u>**Income**</u>

___ rights to the play (if applicable)   ___ donations

___ royalties   ___ concessions

___ photocopies of the script (if legal to do so)   ___ ticket sales

___ publicity   ___ fund raiser
      1) posters
      2) radio   ___ community
      3) invitations
      4) printing   ___ cast
      5) newspapers
                              ___ church

___ set/scenery
      1) lumber   ___ freewill offering
      2) paint
      3) hardware   ___ other _____

___ costumes
      1) rental
      2) material

___ makeup (page 48)

___ props

___ tickets (If you are charging admission or needed to plan for seating)

___ lighting
      1) added spots
      2) gels
      3) installation equipment
      4) hardware

___ programs

___ sound
      1) microphones
      2) sound effects

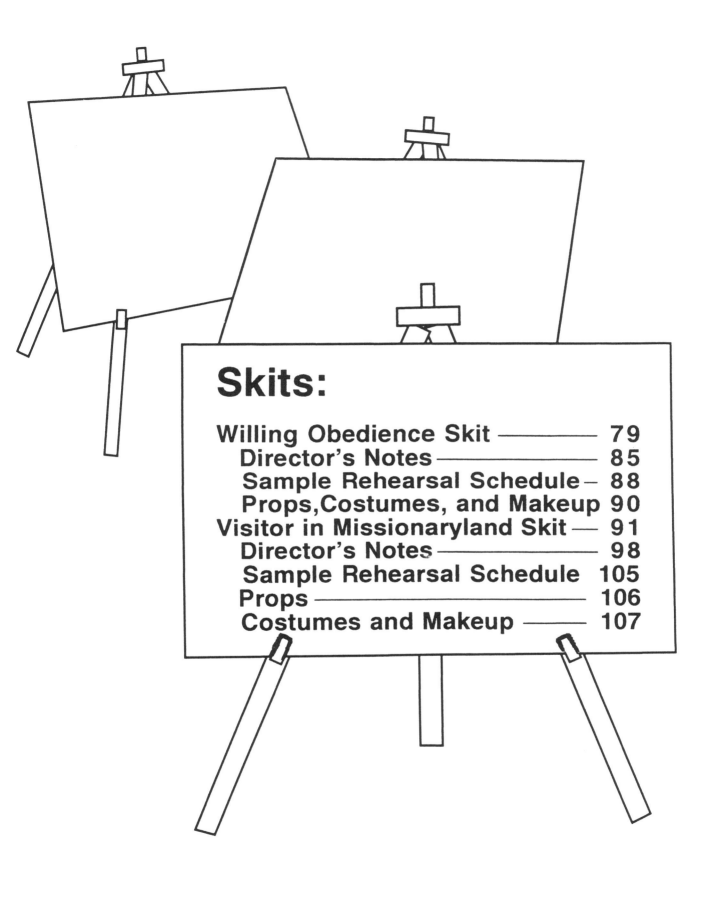

Skits:

WILLING
OBEDIENCE

Willing Obedience Skit

Overview: Old Dog is educating his class of Student Pups and the audience on the subject of Willing Obedience. As Old Dog is teaching the class, the past is relived by the Master and Young Pup who act out his story. The Young Pup's physical expression and the Old Dog's verbal expressions are the real keys to making this skit come alive. This skit may be done by one actor as a monologue.

Characters: **Old Dog** - acts as the narrator for the skit. He is understanding and patient. Using the wisdom he has gained by learning the "hard" way, he shares the lessons he has learned with his Students Pups.

Master - portrays loving authority; the Master is always calm, kind, and patient

Young Pup - is a good puppy, but tries too hard in his own understanding to be obedient, and his emotions get in the way

Ole Tom - older cat who entices Young Pup from obedience and distracts Young Pup's attention

Student Pups - (optional) listen eagerly to Old Dog and interact occasionally with each other

* *

Scene One

Setting: Old Dog downstage right, standing in front of the podium.
Student Pups on floor down front (see diagram page 87).
Leave plenty of room for Master and Young Pup to be
visible as they move around the stage.
(lights up)

(Old Dog speaking to audience. Old Dog clears throat, begins speaking slowly and clearly with gentle authority. Master and Young Pup act out the words of Old Dog. Master and Young Pup NEVER speak.)

Old Dog: I've come here today to talk to you pups about willing obedience. Does anyone have any idea what willing obedience is? *(call on one or more who raise their hand(s) to answer)* Good (or right)! Willing obedience is doing what you're told, but that's only <u>half</u> of obedience. You must obey gladly *without* complaining or protest. Now, I know what you're thinking, *(pause)* I remember when I was a young pup just like you. . . I didn't want to be obedient either! I just wanted to play.

80

Willing Obedience Skit (continued)

(enter Master and Young Pup)

Master & Young Pup:
(Young Pup prances in eagerly with toy. Master attaches leash to collar and puts toy away. Young Pup looks sad and puzzled. Master and Young Pup act out what is spoken by Old Dog. Master always in control and patient, Young Pup over exaggerates all his movements and facial responses.)

Old Dog: The first lesson was when my Master said "Come".

Master & Young Pup:
(Master pats hand on his leg to call Young Pup)

Old Dog: I dragged my feet, whined, howled, and pulled back with all my might!

Master & Young Pup:
(Master waits patiently for Young Pup to quit pulling)

Old Dog: Finally, I realized I was getting nowhere so I looked up at Him.

Master & Young Pup:
(Young Pup looks up. Master pats him on top of his head, while Young Pup thinks about what just happened.)

Old Dog: Patiently again, the Master said "Come".

Master & Young Pup:
(Master again pats hand on leg, calling Young Pup to him)

Old Dog: I got it!

Master & Young Pup:
(Young Pup snaps his fingers, puts finger to side of head while Master nods and smiles.)

Old Dog: Or so I thought! The Master wanted me to go *with* Him and not lag behind! So, eager to please, I darted off full speed ahead.

Master & Young Pup:
(Young Pup bolts forward--Master stands patiently)   81

Willing Obedience Skit (continued)

Old Dog: When I reached the end of that leash . . . WOOF! What a mistake!

Master & Young Pup:
(dazed, Young Pup rolls his head around in circles with tongue hanging out and eyes rolling)

Old Dog: I realized that racing ahead of my Master, even with good intentions, wasn't being obedient either. I wondered if I'd ever learn. Lovingly, my Master said again, "Come".

Master & Young Pup:
(Master pats hand on leg for the third time)

Old Dog: This time I looked up at Him first.

Master & Young Pup:
(Young Pup looks up at Master, who praises him with pats)

Old Dog: Cautiously, I walked beside Him ... looking at Him time and time again.

Master & Young Pup:
(Young Pup looks dubiously up at Master several times, then they proceed to walk around the stage together.)

* *

Scene Two

Setting: Scene break is inserted here to simplify blocking rehearsal. Stage does not change.

Old Dog: Everything seemed O.K. so I became a little bolder...

Master & Young Pup:
(Young Pup gets bolder. Proudly holds head up high, not looking at his Master as much.)

Old Dog: ... and soon I was feeling quite proud of myself.

Willing Obedience Skit (continued)

Master & Young Pup:
(Young Pup struts beside Master who is smiling down at him and encouraging him with pats on the head.)

Old Dog:
Then, out of the corner of my eye, I noticed something move.

(enter Ole Tom)

Old Dog:
It was Ole Tom the cat. I quickly glanced at that old cat... *(pause)*

Ole Tom:
(Ole Tom slowly strolls by Young Pup)

Old Dog:
Then I <u>really</u> looked at him... *(pause)*

Ole Tom:
(Ole Tom taunts Young Pup by sticking out his tongue)

Old Dog:
Forgetting my Master I leaped at Ole Tom!

(Ole Tom jumps up and exits running)

Old Dog:
Do you know what happened when I reached the end of that leash? *(let audience answer; if they don't respond quickly continue with the next line, answering for them)* You're right! WOOF AGAIN! This time I was upset.

Master & Young Pup:
(Young Pup looks up resentfully and grumbles to himself.)

Old Dog:
I had been good. I just wanted to get Ole Tom! I wasn't asking for too much! I pouted.

Master & Young Pup:
(Young Pup crosses arms across chest emphatically and sticks out bottom lip.)

Old Dog:
I looked up at my Master with hurt feelings and anger. "Why me?" I asked. I had tried so hard to be obedient. "He is asking too much of me," I growled.

Willing Obedience Skit (continued)

Master & Young Pup:
> *(Young Pup continues to pout. Master pats and encourages him until pup feels better.)*

Old Dog: Or was He asking too much after all?

Master & Young Pup:
> *(Young Pup cheers up)*

Old Dog: Lovingly and with patience, my Master kept training me.

Master & Young Pup:
> *(Young Pup and Master exit)*

Older Dog: I learned to look up to my Master continually, not lagging behind His will or racing ahead of Him. I learned to be content and obedient following my Master. I was no longer distracted by my own desires, like chasing Ole Tom the cat. And do you know what? Even though I had to give up my own ideas and plans, I was able to go places and do so many more things because I was obedient! Now I really enjoy the outings and adventures my Master plans for me. The love and patience my Master has shown toward me have melted my anger and hurt feelings into willing obedience. Won't you willingly decide to follow your Master today?

(lights out)

THE END

Published by Eternal Hearts

Willing Obedience - Director's Notes

AUDITIONS:

1) Review character guidelines below.
2) Watch for strengths and weaknesses in actors.
3) Choose an actor for each character.

CASTING:

Old Dog:

Needs to speak with authority, knowledge, and understanding. He speaks from experience and relives his feelings, so his speech is not a monologue, but expressive. Must have good physical gestures. Lots of lines to memorize.

Master:

Has confident authority, is calm, and always patient. Watch for actions; fidgety actors will have a harder time portraying Master but can, with practice and good direction, do the job. Facial expressions not as important as physical "stance" of leadership. Look for large hand motions when calling Young Pup. Must be taller than Young Pup.

Young Pup:

He is the focal point that brings alive Old Dog's message. He must be energetic, yet not hyper. Must be a good listener, as he needs to follow with actions what Old Dog speaks. Good facial expression and physical gestures.

Ole Tom:

He is a tempting vice to Young Pup. He antagonizes and lures Young Pup from Master. He needs to have good physical animation and vivid facial expressions, with a mischievous air of sly conceit.

Student Pups (Optional):

Need to respond to Old Dog's questions and occasionally interact among themselves.

85

Willing Obedience - Director's Notes

BLOCKING REHEARSALS:

1) Follow guidelines in the script.

2) Make sure the actors are always visible and their movements on stage are as interesting as possible without being awkward or looking chaotic.

3) As Director, make sure set is positioned so as not to block the view from _any_ seat in the audience. It is common for a Director to watch only from the middle of the first row. This is probably fine in a small setting, but in a large church the perspective will change dramatically and should be considered.

4) It is _very_ common for a Director to have an idea about blocking for a scene only to find out at the rehearsal that it must be adapted. Don't panic - this is normal. Be flexible!

BLOCKING GUIDELINES FOR CHARACTERS:

Old Dog -
> stands on the corner of the stage, talking to the audience and Student Pups

Master -
> leads Young Pup around the stage

Young Pup -
> may walk beside the Master on two legs

Ole Tom -
> Ole Tom stands and calls (finger call) Young Pup over to him, then, sticks tongue out at him

Student Pups -
> 1) may be placed in front of Old Dog on stage
>
> 2) may sit in the front row of the audience

Willing Obedience - Director's Notes

BLOCKING OPTION #1

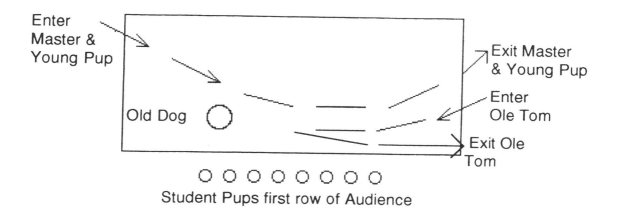

Enter Master & Young Pup

Exit Master & Young Pup

Enter Ole Tom

Exit Ole Tom

Old Dog

Student Pups first row of Audience

BLOCKING OPTION #2

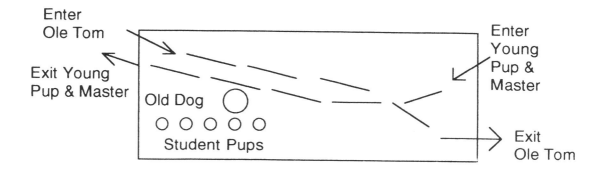

Enter Ole Tom

Exit Young Pup & Master

Enter Young Pup & Master

Exit Ole Tom

Old Dog

Student Pups

Willing Obedience
Sample Rehearsal Schedule

Willing Obedience Rehearsal Plan for Longer Production Time

1) Audition/production crew meeting
2) Read through/discuss feeling and purpose/describe scenes

(Allow enough time to memorize lines for Scene 1 before going on to #3)

3) Scene 1 block, walk through three to four times
4) Review Scene 1, memorize lines Scene 2, Block Scene 2, walk through three to four times

(props/scenery must be complete and in by _____)

5) Run through entire skit until all actors know where and when to move. If ready, start working on detail and polish.
6) Final polish - includes bows, working out any awkward areas or places that the characters do not feel confident
7) Dress Rehearsal and run through two to three times. Don't overkill for perfection.
8) Performance

Willing Obedience Rehearsal Plan for Shorter Production Time

1) Audition/production crew meeting/read through and discuss feeling and purpose. Describe set.

(Allow enough time to memorize script before going on to #2)

2) Block Scene 1 - run through enough times to build actors' confidence about where and when to move
   Block Scene 2 - run through until actors are confident and have mastered the blocking
   Review Scene 1 and 2 together

(props/scenery must be done by this time)

3) Run through and polish, including bows. Work on any uncertain areas identified by either the Director or the actors.
4) Dress rehearsal - run through two to three times. Don't overdo for perfection
5) Performance

Willing Obedience
Rehearsal Schedule

(Come to rehearsal with Scene 1 memorized)

Mon May 4   7-8:30   Rm 129   Block Scene 1
                                 Old Dog, Master
                                 Young Pup, Student Pups

(Come to next rehearsal with Scen 2 memorized)

Mon May 11   7-8:30   Rm 129   Block Scene 2
                                 Review Scene 1
                                 Entire Cast

Thur May 14 7-8:30   Rm 129   Run through Scene 1 and 2
                                 Entire cast

Mon May 18   7-8:30   Sanctuary Review and refine

Thur May 21 7-8:30   Sanctuary Run through
                                 Entire cast and
                                 production crews

Fri May 22 7-9:30   Sanctuary Dress Rehearsal
                                 Entire cast and
                                 production crews

Sat May 23 7:00 pm   Sanctuary Performance

Sun May 24 7:00 pm   Sanctuary Performance

89

Willing Obedience

PROPS: dog leash

SET/SCENERY: podium

The following costume and makeup ideas are for your convenience. Use those ideas that will work for you. It is your production, be creative and have fun!

COSTUMES:

Young Pup -
dressed as a puppy, with either matching brown or black shirt and pants, floppy ears, mittens for paws,
collar options are: 1) use a belt and glue on gaudy stones that will be visible from the audience.
2) place collar around the actor's neck but attach the leash to his clothing to avoid choking

Old Dog -
same as Young Pup above but heavier and older with graying fur

Student Pups -
dress in floppy ears, mittens on hands for paws, have a variety of colors for different pups

Master -
white pants and white dress shirt or white coveralls

Ole Tom -
black leotard and tights (or pants), black pointy ears, long black tail, black mittens

MAKEUP:

Young Pup -
heavy eye makeup, whiskers (either painted or made of pipe cleaners) brown or black patch painted over one eye

Old Dog -
same as Young Pup above but older. Add some gray and wrinkles.

Student Pups -
variations of Young Pup above (may have patches if you like)

Ole Tom -
heavy black eye makeup, false eyelashes, whiskers

Master -
basic makeup as described in this book (pages 49 - 54)

VISITOR

IN

MISSIONARYLAND

Visitor in Missionaryland Skit

Overview: The purpose of this skit is to credit missionaries for their unselfishness and commitment to those they serve. The naive, good-hearted visitor hopes to "save the world". Her pie-in-the-sky vision shatters when reality becomes evident and she finds the life of a missionary very difficult. Yet in the end, God does honor her heart's desire to serve Him--not in her way but His!

Characters:
    Visitor - (young, good-hearted, and naive, must have good facial expressions and physical gestures)
    Missionary - (any age adult, sweet and mellow, yet bold when necessary)
    Market Seller - (any age adult, shrewd, good expressions and body language)
    Thief (1 or 2) - (any age, good physical gestures)
    Thief's Family - (as many extras as you have)*
    Market Scene people - (optional)*
Thief's Family and Market Scene people may be played by same actors

* *

Scene One

Setting: Missionary hut
    Cot at center stage left
    Table and chairs center stage
    Crate in corner upstage right
    (Lights up)

(Visitor sitting on cot pretends to be writing while speaking the opening lines)

Visitor: Dear Diary, Oct. 13,1981 *(performance date)*. Arrived at the village of <u>Two by Two</u> at 10:00 pm. Met Josephine--what a wonderful lady. Arrived at our *(pause)* house *(her voice holds a questioning note)* after a long bumpy ride. It's all so exciting! I can hardly wait to start the Lord's work--passing out tracts, explaining salvation... *(sigh)* Well, I'd better get to sleep.

(Lies down to go to sleep and pauses 10 seconds. Lights dim. Lights up as she gets up, stretches, and takes a deep breath. As the visitor begins looking around the room, first haphazardly, then more seriously, the missionary enters.)

Visitor: Good morning, Josephine. *(may use name of actor)*

Missionary: Good morning, Vonnie. *(may use name of actor)* What are you looking for? Did you lose something?   92

Visitor in Missionaryland Skit (continued)

Visitor: No ... I was going to start breakfast but ... *(pauses to glance around the room one last time)* I - I can't find the refrigerator!

Missionary: *(chuckling)* It's no wonder, my dear. I don't have a refrigerator! Refrigerators are not common here in <u>Two by Two</u>!

Visitor: Oh ... *(looking a little relieved, then concerned)* what do you do then?

Missionary: Come ... I'll show you! *(both exit, lights out)*

* Option - If you are doing this in a regular room, you may set up the hut scene at one side and the market scene at the other side of the room.

* *

Scene Two

Setting: Market setting.
Seller's booth, table with crates of oranges, eggs, etc. upstage right
Crates set downstage right for visitor to sit on

(Lights on)

Visitor: The market place. Of course!

Missionary: Yes, we shop every morning. Here is a peso. Why don't you buy us a few oranges, while I get some things for dinner. *(walks to market area)*

Visitor: Sure! *(walks toward orange stand) (speaks slowly with much effort)* I'd like oranges please. *(Seller doesn't understand and looks confused. Visitor picks up an orange to show him or her)*

Seller: *(Seller asks "How much?")* Quanta cuesta?

Visitor: *(Visitor, not understanding the language, stutters a reply of what she thinks is the right amount)* Ah... ah... one peso.

Visitor in Missionaryland Skit (continued)

Seller: One peso? *(surprised but very pleased)*

Visitor: *(proudly)* Yes! One peso!

Seller: Ah ... si. *(smiles big as he fills a large sack with oranges, while Visitor's expression turns from pleasure to dismay)*

Visitor: Grac-i-as *(unenthusiastically)* *(Seller plays with coin as Visitor walks away)*

(Visitor sets sack down and sits on crate in corner to wait for the Missionary. Missionary enters)

Missionary: Well, dear, were you able to get us some oranges?

Visitor: Yes, *(turns around and picks up the huge bag full)* and then some! *(smiles sheepishly as she holds up the bag)*

Missionary: *(chuckles, puts her arm around the Visitor's shoulder)* Come, I'll show you how it's done here!

(both walk back to seller)

[The following scenario is an example of an ad-lib as described on page 57. It may or may not be used in the skit.
(The Missionary accidentally steps on Visitor's shoe. Visitor trips. Missionary reaches out to steady the Visitor.)
Missionary: Are you all right, Dear?
Visitor: Certainly, just a rock in my shoe!
(They continue walking to Seller's booth.)]

(Visitor stands back between the Seller and Missionary, turning her head back and forth, as Missionary and Seller dicker over the price of eggs.)

Missionary: Eggs? How much?

Seller: 1 peso

Missionary: Too much--50 centavos!

Seller: No! No! No! I have much family to feed. *(hands fly emotionally)* 80 centavos!

Missionary: 65 centavos and no more!   94

Visitor in Missionaryland Skit (continued)

Seller: (pauses, scrutinizing whether Missionary will bid higher, then decides to agree)
Si, Si.

(Missionary pays and hands tract to the seller. Two walk off triumphantly back home while Seller looks over tract then throws it away)
(lights out or exit back around to hut scene)

* *

Scene Three

Setting: Missionary hut (same as Scene one)
(lights on)

(back home, Visitor is putting away food in or on crate in corner)

Visitor: Oh! ...(jumping back from the crate) What's that?

Missionary: Oh, dear! I should have warned you ... (as she disposes of bug) we tend to have a bit of a bug problem here. Ants in the sugar, cockroaches and spiders most everywhere. Don't worry, you'll get used to their surprises.

(Visitor looks toward audience with extremely dubious expression and mouths "I don't think so", as she shakes her head)

Missionary: Well, it's siesta time. (Missionary exits)

Visitor: (Visitor sits on cot with diary) I am tired and it is so...
(Visitor jumps up quickly to check for bugs. With relief she reseats herself) hot!

(Visitor lies down to nap and is molested by mosquitoes. She swats continually at the air. Finally, Visitor triumphs over bug and sleeps 10 seconds.)

("Flight of the Bumble Bee" is a great sound effect or record buzzing noises.)

(Missionary enters with dinner on a tray.)

Missionary: Wake up, sleepyhead. Here's dinner. Since it's your first night here, I thought you'd enjoy a native delicacy called Balut. (sets tray on the table)

95

Visitor in Missionaryland Skit (continued)

Visitor: M-m-m. Sounds great! *(enthusiastically)* What is it?!

Missionary: Oh, it's a duck egg that was buried so the baby wasn't able to hatch. *(Visitor looks aghast.)* It's quite tasty.

Visitor: I'm sure it is, but ... *(pauses to think of an excuse not to eat it)* with the heat today, I'm not so hungry tonight ... If you don't mind I think I'll *(looks quickly around the room for something)* have an orange!

Missionary: Well, whatever you think is best.

Visitor: Yes, believe me, it really is best. *(says assuredly)*

Missionary: O.K. I need to run these Bibles to the people in the barrio...

Visitor: Oh! Can I help? *(excitedly)*

Missionary: No... not this time. I think it's best if you stay here, if you don't mind.

Visitor: No. *(dejectedly)* I don't mind.
(Missionary exits)

Visitor: *(toward audience)* Well, let's see if I can find something to eat. I'm starving! *(exits)*

Music - Pink Panther, Mission Impossible theme or some other spy theme

   (One Thief enters, looks around, backs into visitor coming in with oranges. Both jump in surprise.)
   (Two thieves can do a slapstick routine by separating and then backing into each other, thus startling each other as Visitor enters.)

Visitor: What can I do for you?

Thief: Hm-m-m *(Thief hems and haws)* *(two thieves hem and haw looking awkwardly at each other)*

Visitor: *(catches onto the situation and plays dumb.)* Oh, here, have something to eat. We have some Balut left over from dinner and we have lots of oranges. *(Thief, Thieves look dumbfounded)* You did come to learn about Jesus. Right?

96

Visitor in Missionaryland Skit (continued)

Thief: *(one thief Nods head yes) (two thieves look at each other and nod a very exaggerated "Yes!")*

Visitor: Wait, while I get my Bible. *(Visitor looks up and clasps hands.)* Thank you, Lord. *(exits)*

(Thief(ves) runs out immediately after she exits)

(Visitor comes back, looks around, then realizes that thief(ves) have vanished. She is utterly devastated. Plops into chair with diary.)

Visitor: Today has not gone <u>ex-act-ly</u> as I thought it would. I had hoped for ...

(Knock on door, visitor gestures like "now what", opens door and in comes thief(ves) with entire family.)

Thief: *(with a large grin, heavy accent with broken english)* You so kind, nice lady, I get my whole family to know Jesus, too! *(family nod their heads enthusiastically in agreement)*

Visitor: Come in! Come in! *(ushers everyone in ahead of her)* Make yourselves at home *(looks around, walks to crate and offers oranges)*--have some oranges.

(oranges passed to all actors, Missionary enters)

Missionary: What's going on here? *(in disbelief)*

Visitor: *(beaming)* They'd all like to know Jesus!

Missionary: Come, I'll tell you all about Him.

(All exit except Visitor, she walks back over to her diary and picks it up and begins to write.)

Visitor: Dear Diary, I was wrong! This day was more than I had hoped for! *(looks up)* Thank you, Lord *(looks down, then quickly back up)*--and God ... thanks for the oranges.
                  (lights out)

THE END

                               Published by Eternal Hearts

Visitor In Missionaryland - Director's Notes

AUDITIONS:

1) Review character guidelines below
2) Watch for strengths and weaknesses in actors
3) Choose actor for each character

CASTING:

Visitor - good facial and body expressions; air of innocence
Missionary - has a poised calm about her, has an inner strength

Thief(ves) - look for good pantomime gestures, with large exaggerated movements

Seller - look for animated actions, boldness

Thief's Family/Market people - variety of personalities

BLOCKING REHEARSALS:

(Stage directions have been given assuming that you have a stage with wings. Adapt as needed, making sure that you exit and enter from the left or right side of the stage as directed if possible.)

1) Director must be thoroughly familiar with the script. Do not go into blocking rehearsals without any ideas. Have at least a general plan.

2) Follow guidelines in the script.

3) Make sure the actors are always visible and their movements on stage are as interesting as possible without being awkward or looking chaotic.

4) As Director make sure set is positioned so as not to block the view from <u>any</u> seat, in the audience. It is common for a Director to watch only from the middle of the first row. This is probably fine in a small setting, but in a large church the perspective will change dramatically and should be considered.

5) It is <u>very</u> common for a Director to have an idea for blocking a scene, only to find out at the rehearsal that it must be adapted. Don't panic - this is normal. Be flexible!

Visitor In Missionaryland - Director's Notes

BLOCKING SCENE 1

M = Missionary
V = Visitor
T = Thief 1
TT = Thief 2
1 = 1st move
2 = 2nd move

MOVES: Visitor 1 - wakes up at cot, looks around, and walks to crate
Missionary 1 - enters downstage left and crosses to Visitor
    standing by crate
Visitor & Missionary 2 - exit downstage right together

SCENE 1

```
┌─────────────────────────────────────────────────────────────┐
│                                                               │
│   CRATE                                                       │
│     ☐   V1                           V1      ┌───────────┐   │
│                                              │    COT    │   │
│   Exit        M1                             └───────────┘   │
│   V2                                              V          │
│                                                               │
│       M2   CHAIR  ┌──────────┐  CHAIR         M1            │
│              ☐    │  TABLE   │   ☐                          │
│   M2              └──────────┘                              │
│   Exit                                     Enter          M │
│                                            downstage        │
│                                            left             │
└─────────────────────────────────────────────────────────────┘
```

AUDIENCE

PROPS: _ cot
_ crates
_ table
_ 2 chairs
_ diary
_ pillow
_ blanket
_ pen

Visitor In Missionaryland - Director's Notes

BLOCKING SCENE 2

MOVES:

1 Visitor & Missionary - enter downstage left and cross to center

2 Missionary - moves to market area upstage left
   Visitor - moves to Seller's table to buy oranges

3 Visitor - moves to crate after oranges are purchased
   Missionary - moves to crate after talking to market people

4 Visitor & Missionary - move together to Seller's table, Visitor follows behind and moves to back corner of Seller's table

5 Visitor & Missionary - exit downstage left

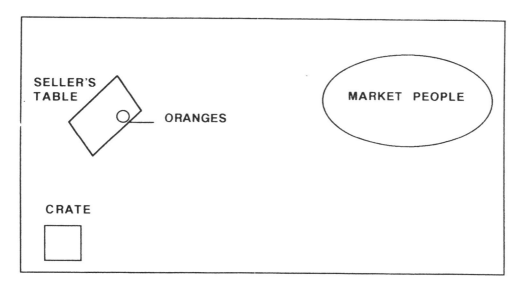

PROPS:
_ Bible tract
_ peso
_ eggs
_ crates
_ table for Seller
_ various produce for sale
_ oranges
_ large bag for oranges
_ various market objects such as baskets and food (If available you could even have a parrot in a cage)

Visitor In Missionaryland - Director's Notes

BLOCKING SCENE 3

(Scene 3 is divided into three sections as so many moves are involved)

MOVES:
Missionary and Visitor 1 - enter downstage right
Visitor 2 - crosses to crate, puts oranges on crate
Missionary 2 - exits center stage left
Visitor 3 - crosses to cot to take a nap
Missionary 3 - enters center stage left and walks to table, sets tray on table and sits down in chair
Visitor 4 - crosses to table and sits down in chair
Missionary 5 - exits downstage right
Visitor 5 - exits downstage right

CRATE

COT

CHAIR   CHAIR

TABLE

M   V

BLOCKING SCENE 3 (CONT)

MOVES: (Option 1 two thieves)

Thieves 1 - enter center stage right, one walks to crate, the other walks to cot

(Option 2 one thief)

Thief 1 - enters center stage right, walks to cot and looks under, walks to crate and looks in

(Option 1 two thieves)

Thieves 2 - they back towards each other and bump into each other center stage by table

Visitor 1 - enters downstage left, crosses to table not seeing thief

Thief 2 - backs up towards table and startles Visitor

Visitor 2 - exits downstage left

Thieves 2 - exits downstage right

Visitor 3 - enters downstage left

Visitor 4 - moves to chair and plops down with diary

Visitor In Missionaryland - Director's Notes

BLOCKING SCENE 3 (CONT)

MOVES:
1 Visitor - walks to center stage right and lets thief and family in through pretend door (door is optional)
2 Visitor - moves to crate
1 Thief and family - enters center stage right, move to table area
1 Missionary - enters center stage right
2 Thief and family - exit to center stage left
2 Missionary - exits center stage left with thief and family
3 Visitor - moves to table

PROPS: same as Scene 1 with the following additions

_ 2 ceramic dishes
_ utensils
_ serving dish with lid for Balut
_ large plastic bug (is optional)
_ bag of oranges
_ stack of Bibles

CURTAIN CALL: reappearance order of the cast for bows

1) Family and Market People
2) Seller and Thieves
3) Missionary and Visitor

Visitor In Missionaryland - Director's Notes

CRATE

COT

CHAIR | TABLE | CHAIR

CRATE

COT

CHAIR | TABLE | CHAIR

CRATE

COT

CHAIR | TABLE | CHAIR

104

Visitor In Missionaryland
Sample Rehearsal Schedule

(Come to rehearsal with Scene 1 memorized)

Mon April 20	7-8:30	Rm 129	Block Scene 1 Visitor & Missionary

(Come to next rehearsal with Scene 2 memorized)

Mon April 27	7-8:30	Rm 129	Block Scene 2 Run through Scene 1 & 2 Visitor, Missionary, Seller, & crowd if using

(Come to next rehearsal with Scene 3 memorized)

Mon May 4	7-8:30	Rm 129	Block Scene 3 Run through Scenes 1,2,3 Entire cast
Mon May 11	7-8:30	Rm 129	Run through entire play two times (three if possible) Entire cast
Thur May 14	7-8:30	Rm 129	Run through entire play two to three times Entire cast
Mon May 18	7-8:30	Rm 129	Run through entire play
Thur May 21	7-8:30	Sanctuary	Run through Entire cast & production crews
Fri May 22	7-9:30	Sanctuary	Dress Rehearsal Entire cast & production crews
Sat May 23	7:00 pm	Sanctuary	Performance
Sun May 24	7:00 pm	Sanctuary	Performance

Visitor in Missionaryland

PROP CHECKLIST:

Scene 1:
_ diary
_ pen
_ old wood table
_ 2 - 4 chairs
_ cot
_ blanket
_ pillow
_ crates

Scene 2:
_ Bible tract
_ peso/penny
_ eggs
_ crates
_ table for Seller
_ various produce for sale
_ oranges
_ large bag for oranges (preferably see through)
_ various market objects such as baskets and food
(we actually had a parrot in a cage)

Scene 3:
_ diary
_ pen
_ old wood table
_ 2 - 4 chairs
_ cot
_ blanket
_ pillow
_ crates
_ two ceramic dishes
_ utensils
_ serving dish with lid for Balut
_ large plastic bug (if you desire or can just pretend)
_ tray
_ bag of oranges
_ stack of Bibles
_ Bible

Visitor in Missionaryland

COSTUMES:

Visitor - modern summer dress, or culottes/shorts, tennis shoes or sandals

Missionary - clean colorful skirt, white South American style blouse, sandals

Thief - old, ragged, South American style shirt, shorts or tattered jeans, sandals

Thief's Family - old, clean but ragged clothes, sandals

Seller - (man) straw hat, white long-sleeve shirt, rolled-up sleeves, baggy pants, sandals (woman) straw hat, skirt, blouse, sandals

Market People - South American sombreros or straw hats, colorful South American clothes, sandals

MAKEUP: To apply makeup, follow instructions in the chapter 6 of this book.

Visitor - very light complexion

Missionary - dark tan complexion

All others - very dark complexion

Resources

BOOKS:

The books below are available through the "King County" library system in Seattle,WA, though they may not be available at your local library. Do not be discouraged if a book is not available to you, as there are many books on the subjects below. Your new understanding of drama gives you the knowledge to find the information you need in other sources, or order these through the inter library system from King County, WA library.

Acting and Audition Helps:

Finchly, Joan, Audition! A complete guide for actors with an annotated selection of readings. Englewood Cliffs, NJ: Prentice-Hall, Inc., 1984

Bernarde, Philip, Improvisation Starters A collection of 900 improvisation situations for the theater. White Hall, VA: Betterway Publications, Inc., 1992
Good for actors to learn how to ad-lib.

Hobbs, William, Stage Fright. New York, NY: Theatre Arts Book, 1967
Teaches you the special steps and techniques to perform sword fights, fisticuffs, firearms, and slapstick without injury to yourself or fellow man.

Black, David, The Actor's Audition Finally - the technique book on the art of auditions. New York, NY: Vintage Books, 1990
This is a great little book on how to audition!

Cassady, Marshall, The Book of Scenes for Acting Practice. Lincolnwood, IL: National Textbook Co., 1985
This book gives you a variety of style, characters, and types of drama to sharpen you acting skills.

Costumes:

Cummings, Richard, 101 Costumes for All Ages, All Occasions. Boston, MA: Plays, Inc., 1987

Cassin-Scott, Jack, Costumes and Setting for Staging Historical Plays
Volumes 1-4 Boston, MA: Plays, Inc., 1979
Each volume covers a certain time period. Volume 1 covers the Classical Period, Volume 2 covers Medieval Period, Volume 3 The Elizabethan and Restoration Period, and Volume 4 the Georgian Period. These volumes not only include costume ideas (with hair and makeup), but props, set designs, and even a play title list from that particular time period.

Jackson, Sheila, <u>Costumes for the Stage</u> A complete handbook for every kind of play. New York, NY: Dutton Pub, 1978
A great book to sew your own costumes or look through the book for ideas of different time period clothing. See other titles written by her also.

Motley, <u>Designing and Making Stage Costumes</u>. New York, NY: Watson-Guptill Publications, 1964

Lighting:

Parker, W. Oren and Wolff, R. Craig, <u>Stage Lighting</u>: Practice and Design. New York, NY: Holt, Rinehart and Winston, 1987
Has great pictures in the center section of the book about lighting placement and its effect on the stage and the actors.

Boulanger, Norman C. and Lounsburg, Warren C., <u>Theatre Lighting from A-Z</u>. Seattle, WA: University of Washington Press, 1992
This book is basically an encyclopedia about the essential equipment, techniques, and concepts of stage lighting. Great drawings and diagrams. Probably more information than you'll ever need, but worth a look.

Makeup:

Dalla Palma, Diego, <u>Makeup Artists Handbook for Stages, Screen, and Video</u>. New York, NY: Sterling Publishing Co. Inc., 1985
Includes makeup techniques, period hair styles and makeup, special effects. Excellent book with black and white pictures.

Bruun-Rasmussen, Ole and Petersen, Grete, <u>Make-up, Costumes and Masks for the Stage</u>. New York, NY: Sterling Pub. Co. Inc., 1976
Good beginners book.

Cummings, Richard, <u>Simple Makeup for Young Actors.</u> Boston, MA: Plays, Inc., 1990
This book has a good selection of ideas for the use of putty, wigs, wounds, tattoos, and the creating of different nationalities.

Corson, Richard, <u>Stage Makeup</u>. Englewood Cliffs, NJ: Prentice Hall, Inc., 1989

Jans, Martin, <u>The Art of Doing Stage Make-up Techniques</u>. Kidderminster, Amsterdam: Van Dobbenburgh, 1986
This book has many ideas and color pictures.

Miscellaneous Books:

Jennings, Coleman A. and Harris, Aurand, <u>Plays Children Love Volume II</u>: A
treasury of contemporary and classic plays for children. New York,
NY: St. Martins Press, 1981
Plays include: Charlottes' Web, Treasure Island, The Best
Christmas Pageant Ever. Part 1 is written for adult actors and
Part II is for children to perform.

Pryor, Nick, <u>Putting on a Play</u>. New York, NY: Thomson Learning, 1994
An easy book for younger children to read and comprehend all
aspects of drama. It is very succinct and full of wonderful pictures.

Alberts, David, <u>Talking about Mime</u>: An illustrated guide. Portsmouth, NH:
Heinemann, 1994
Nice basic book on mime that includes pictures and nicely
described do's and don'ts.

Stage, Set Construction, and Props:

Govier, Jacquie, <u>Create Your Own Stage Props</u>. Englewood Cliffs, NJ:
Prentice-Hall, Inc., 1984
An excellent book describing a wide variety of materials including
wood, wire, paper mache, and more. The first section of the book
teaches techniques and tools (like brushes). The second section
gives some step-by-step instructions to make your own props.

Miller, James Hull, <u>Self-supporting Scenery for Children's Theatre.and Grown-
ups too</u>: A scenic workbook for the open stage. (fourth edition)
Downers Grove, IL: Meriwether Pub., Inc., 1982

Lord, William H., <u>Stagecraft 1</u>: A complete guide to backstage work. Colorado
Springs, CO: Meriwether Pub., Inc., 1991
This book includes information on stages and rigging, production
staff, props, sound, and set construction.

Kenton, Warren, <u>Stage Properties and How to Make Them</u>. New York, NY:
Pitman, 1978

Southern, Richard, <u>Stage Setting for Amateurs and Professionals</u>. London,
England: Faber and Faber, 1964
A good book on stage construction, but more complex than most
will need.

James, Thurston, <u>The Prop Builder's Molding and Casting Handbook</u>. White
Hall, VA: Betterway Publications, Inc., 1989
A comprehensive guide in using molding and casting materials to
make props.

Beck, Roy A., <u>Stagecraft.</u> (third edition) Lincolnwood, IL: National Textbook Co.,
1990
This is a nice, succinct and easy to follow book covering scenery
construction, lighting, and sound.

Play Publishers:

✓Baker's Plays
100 Chauncy Street
Boston, MA 02111-1783
Phone: 1-617-482-1280
Includes: historical pageants for holiday celebrations, short easily
produced contemporary pieces for worship service, plays for
youngsters and adults, plays for discussion aids, and professional
productions.

✓Continental Ministries/The Jeremiah Group
425 West 115th Ave
Denver, CO 80234
Phone: 1-805-289-3450
Comedy sketches and monologues

✓ Genevox Music Group
127 Ninth Ave. North
Nashville, TN 37234
Phone: 1-800-436-3869
Dramas and Musicals with drama included.

✓Good News Music Service
10415 Beardslee Blvd.
Bothel, WA. 98011-3271
1-800-821-9207
Retails drama resources and music

✓ Lillenas Drama Resource
Box 419527
Kansas City, MO. 64141
Phone: 1-800-877-0700

> Excellent selection of plays including: full length and one act plays. Sketch collections for youth and adults, plays for schools, and dinner theaters. Worship drama, monologues, and more.

✓ Plays, Inc.
120 Boylston
Boston MA 02116
Phone: 1-617-423-3157

> A complete source of original plays and programs for school-age actors and audiences. Each issue includes 8-10 plays, arranged by age level (lower grades through Jr. and Sr. High School). Large variety of themes including holidays, history, comedies, mysteries, and many others that are royalty free with paid subscription.

✓ Willow Creek Resources Drama Sketch Singles
5300 Patterson Ave. S.E.
Grand Rapids, MI. 49530
Phone: 1-800-876-7335

> Willow Creek Community Church uses original sketches as part of their weekend services. The target audience is the non-churched and the sketches are not intended to be a preaching tool, but rather to raise questions and/or issues that the pastor can address with biblical truth. The sketches average six minutes in length.

More Options for finding costumes, makeup, props, settings, plays, etc.:

Local Telephone Directories - look up the following headings in your local yellow pages:

> Theatrical Equipment and Supplies
> Theatrical Makeup
> Thrift Stores
> Community Theaters

Internet Web Sites:

The web sites listed below all have plays you may download. Some charge royalties or may be purchased after previewing them first, while some are free. To find these web sites use the URL's listed below or Web Browser to look up the key words "Drama" and "Christian". Then look up the name of the company. (example: The Christian Drama Consortium)

Christian Bits and Pieces
http://www.zeta.org.au/~andrewa/aja451.htm

Drama Ministry Homepage
dmcclellan@comresources.com
1-800-992-2144

The Christian Drama Consortium
haynese@cadvision.com
1-403-246-0290

Makeup Companies:

Ben Nye Co. Inc.
5935 Bowcroft St
Los Angeles, CA 90016
1-310-839-1984

Bob Kelly Cosmetics
151 W 46th S.
New York, NY 10036
1-202-819-0030

Mehron Inc.
100 Red Schoolhouse Rd
Chestnut Ridge, NY 10977
1-800-332-9955

Our Mission

Eternal Hearts is dedicated to creating quality educational products that develop a love for learning. Products that are fun and stress free, affordable, and enjoyed by children and adults alike.

We'd love to hear from you and have you enter our free drawing...

If you have any suggestions, comments, ideas, or stories you would like to share with us regarding Drama Made Easy--or if you have a video of one of the skits you produced from this book, send us a copy. Use one of the forms on the next page to drop us a note. You will be automatically entered into our free drawing to win a copy of our soon to be released play <u>Christmas Thieves</u> (see description below), Rummy Roots card game, or More Roots card game.

Christmas Thieves
A typical American family is <u>busy</u> getting ready for the holiday season when gang members break into their home and steal all their Christmas presents. Through their experience, the Jones learn that the gang members were not the real thieves. Find out who (or what) the real thieves are and how the Jones remake their Christmas without money or store bought presents.

In His Steps, the Play
An adaptation of Charles Sheldon's book <u>In His Steps</u>.
When Rev. Henry Maxwell's morning worship service is interrupted by a sick and dying tramp, the congregations lives and understanding of Christianity are radically changed. Rev Maxwell challenges his congregation to ask "What would Jesus do?" before making <u>any</u> decisions in their personal and professional lives. The subsequent events in the lives of these people will amaze and challenge you in your own walk in life.

Additional Eternal Hearts products:

Rummy Roots
English Vocabulary building card game that teaches 42 Greek and Latin roots in a fun and stress free way. Improves vocabulary and dictionary skills without even being aware you are learning. Child recommended. Ages 8-adult $10.95 +$3.00 shipping & handling

More Roots
Same as above with an additional 42 Greek and Latin roots
$10.95 + $3.00 shipping & handling

Other educational products are available. All products available through your local books store or home school supply; or you may order from:

Eternal Hearts
PO Box 107
Colville, WA 99114
509-732-4147

Comment/Suggestion Card

Eternal Hearts is dedicated to serving your educational needs. Your comments, suggestions, or questions regarding any of our products are welcome. Please use the form provided below or drop us a note.

Sincerely Sandra Everson & Karena Krull

Product Title: _____   _____

Comments/Suggestions/Questions: _____

_____

_____

_____

Name: _____

Address: _____   Mail to: Eternal Hearts

_____   PO Box 107
                                                     Colville, WA 99114
City: _____ State: _____ Zip: _____   (509) 732-4147

☐ Send more information

Comment/Suggestion Card

Eternal Hearts is dedicated to serving your educational needs. Your comments, suggestions, or questions regarding any of our products are welcome. Please use the form provided below or drop us a note.

Sincerely Sandra Everson & Karena Krull

Product Title: _____

Comments/Suggestions/Questions: _____

_____

_____

_____

Name: _____

Address: _____   Mail to: Eternal Hearts

_____   PO Box 107
                                                     Colville, WA 99114
City: _____ State: _____ Zip: _____   (509) 732-4147

☐ Send more information

Comment/Suggestion Card

Eternal Hearts is dedicated to serving your educational needs. Your comments, suggestions, or questions regarding any of our products are welcome. Please use the form provided below or drop us a note.

Sincerely Sandra Everson & Karena Krull

Product Title: _____

Comments/Suggestions/Questions: _____

_____

_____

_____

Name: _____

Address: _____   _____   Mail to: Eternal Hearts
                                                       PO Box 107
City: _____ State: _____ Zip: _____   Colville, WA 99114

☐ Send more information   (509) 732-4147